Praise for *A W*

"A lovely walk through the most magickal of settings, the world of gardens, both domestic and wild. The author is a master gardener who brings together her life practice of wildcrafting and the use of herbs in spells and ritual intentions. Her graceful prose about the practical and the spiritual makes this a fine addition to any library."

—Holli Emore, executive director
of Cherry Hill Seminary

"Walker provides a balance between best practices, scientific knowledge, and decades of herbalist and magical experience. Her knowledge and expertise on herbalism shines in this text. The descriptions of each plant and its use are great for both beginner and advanced practitioners. An incredible resource for anyone, magical or not. A must-have for everyone's bookshelf!"

—Deidre Rogers, adjunct faculty at California Polytechnic
State University, consultant at the Dissertation Coach,
and faculty member at Cherry Hill Seminary in the
Department of Ministry, Advocacy & Leadership

A WITCH'S GUIDE TO

WILDCRAFT

© Paul Church

About the Author

JD Walker (Greensboro, NC) is the vice chancellor of the House of Akasha, a North Carolina Pagan group. A former business journalist, she is currently retired but continues to work as a freelance reporter and she has contributed dozens of articles to Llewellyn's almanacs.

A WITCH'S GUIDE TO

WILDCRAFT

Using

Common

Plants

to Create

Uncommon

Magick

⛤

J D
WALKER

Llewellyn Publications
Woodbury, Minnesota

FIRST EDITION
First Printing, 2021

Cover design by Kevin R. Brown
Maps on pages 82–83 by Llewellyn Art Department
Interior art by Trisha Previte

Llewellyn Publications is a registered trademark of Llewellyn Worldwide Ltd.

Library of Congress Cataloging-in-Publication Data
Names: Walker, J. D., author.
Title: A witch's guide to wildcraft : using common plants to create uncommon magick / JD Walker.
Description: Woodbury, Minnesota : Llewellyn Publications, [2021] | Includes bibliographical references. | Summary: "*A Witch's Guide to Wildcraft* explores more than thirty common North American plants, providing tips for identification, gathering, and cultivation as well as specific rituals and magical uses"— Provided by publisher.
Identifiers: LCCN 2021000464 (print) | LCCN 2021000465 (ebook) | ISBN 9780738765433 (paperback) | ISBN 9780738765594 (ebook)
Subjects: LCSH: Witchcraft. | Magic. | Plants—North America.
Classification: LCC BF1566 .W35 2021 (print) | LCC BF1566 (ebook) | DDC 133.4—dc23
LC record available at https://lccn.loc.gov/2021000464
LC ebook record available at https://lccn.loc.gov/2021000465

Llewellyn Publications
A Division of Llewellyn Worldwide Ltd.
2143 Wooddale Drive
Woodbury, MN 55125-2989
www.llewellyn.com

Printed in the United States of America

Disclaimer

Do not eat, smoke, or consume in any form plants that have been gathered away from your home or locations otherwise out of your control. Do not ingest any of the plants you gather if you don't personally know how you will react to that plant or the life history of that plant. Readers are advised to consult their doctors or other qualified healthcare professionals before taking herbal supplements or remedies. The publisher and the author assume no liability for any injuries caused to the reader that may result from the reader's use of content contained in this publication and recommend common sense when contemplating the practices described in the work.

Contents

Crafting List

Foreword

In my business and metaphysical experience, it has been a challenge trying to find a good down-to-earth reference book on herbs for magickal uses that combines how to identify commonly used plants with the ways to harvest and utilize them. One of the primary focuses in my shop is to offer a wide array of herbs that can assist our practitioners of many spiritual paths. I am always adding more as the clients call for them. And there are a lot of calls.

JD and I met about twenty years ago when she visited my shop, and we found a fast and lasting friendship. She originally came in for the reasons many "explorers" do—to find information and a community of like-minded people. Sources were not as prolific back then, and, believe it or not, the internet was not the information hub it is these days. (My, what twenty years can bring to our lives.) My medical training taught me to be a great phlebotomist and X-ray tech, and my metaphysical training is quite extensive. I truly appreciate the value of herbs and know my way around a cauldron, mojo, and poppet, but I am a brown thumb at best when it comes to plants. My skills with herbs come into play once they are dried. When JD attended one of my herb classes, I quickly learned that she had a vast grasp of how to grow, care for, and identify plant life. Madame Master Gardener (as I sometimes call her) puts me to shame in this regard. Together, JD and I make a damn fine team.

Many years ago, JD and I found ourselves in discussion on how to address the absence of a reference book on common North American plants in the market. It is wonderful to chat about the impact of Middle Eastern resins and African and Central American exotics, but very few of my customers and clients will ever travel to these regions to truly learn about the plants. We decided that she should write a commonsense guidebook on herbs to better assist my Pagan clients.

JD insisted the book had to be about herbs that people could relate to, find nearby, and easily identify. She certainly has the expertise for this kind of project. She has told me many a story about why we grow the stuff we grow, the background of the use of this plant or that, new discoveries about how to use various plants, and more. In fact, my friends and I rib her a bit from time to time when she gets going on the topic.

Now, the publication of such a book is finally happening. I am so proud and happy to see JD's vision realized. This book hits all those marks we considered. *A Witch's Guide to Wildcraft: Using Common Herbs to Create Uncommon Magick* is down to earth: readers anywhere along the Pagan path can read it, understand what is being explained, and apply the information to the plants in their own backyard. The blend of references to old grimoires with more modern metaphysical classics will help the reader go further in their own journey of discovery with herbs.

This is wonderfully insightful information written by a witch who knows her stuff. I think anyone who picks it up will be impressed with it, and I expect it will become a standard on the bookshelves of many a Pagan. A good reference book like this is one you just keep going back to.

Sarah McDavid
High Priestess of House of Akasha
Owner of Terra Blue

Introduction

Herbs. They are part and parcel of most witches' tool chests. Herbalists and Pagan practitioners use them to calm the mind and spirit and to help activate the universe to achieve our goals. One of the best ways to succeed in magick is to really connect with the herbs used. Most average-size cities have at least one herbal store, but there is no better way to really connect with the herbs you intend to use than by personally collecting and processing your own herbs. This is what I call "wildcrafting."

My Life as a Gardener

How would I know this? I've been wildcrafting plants for many years, originally because that was the way I was raised. My parents had nine kids, so my family gardened to supplement the food budget. Oddly, only one of my younger brothers and I grew up to be gardeners. The rest either hire the work out or avoid it like the plague.

We also took advantage of anything edible that grew on the surrounding land. Berries were an obvious food source, but as kids, we snacked on pickleweed and honeysuckle blossoms. We gathered walnuts for Grandma's cakes and pig nuts and acorns for her pigs. We picked creasy greens (wild and cultivated), poke, and ditch daisy blossoms.

As an adult, I continued to cultivate my love of gardening. Soon after settling into my life post-college, I happened on our state's Master Gardener program. I stayed with the program for over five years, learning, volunteering, and helping set up our state Master Gardener Association. One of our main tasks was to man the phones on certain days to field plant questions from area citizens. I frequently found it amusing when consulting with a concerned homeowner about something he or she called a weed to explain to them I used to eat that weed for dinner.

Eventually, I left the nine-to-five world to start my own landscaping business. Along the way, I also indulged my passion for writing, starting a garden column that I continued for almost thirty years.

My Life as a Wildcrafting Witch

My interest in the occult is about as old as my interest in gardening. From the time my mother let me wander the book stacks on my own in the city library, I soon found and devoured every book I could check out on the occult. Our local library must have had a closeted witch or two. It had a surprisingly large selection to choose from.

Mama and Grandma took my interest in stride. They were firm believers in the spirit world, if a little suspicious of the reports that circulated in the late 1960s and '70s of witch cults and so-called devil worshippers. When they realized my interest was more than a child's passing fancy, they kept an eye on me and my reading but let the topic lie. If the conversation ever turned toward the subject, Grandma would just sigh and say, "She's always been a bit quier." That's *queer*, pronounced by my grandmother as "qwhere." It's basically old-world speak for "strange but harmless."

I self-dedicated as a solitary Pagan at a rather difficult point in my life when I was transitioning to a major career change as a professional reporter, ending a long-term relationship, and mourning the loss of my mother. It was a tough time and being in nature was my only solace.

My gardening interests and spiritual practices blended seamlessly. Most Pagans have an affinity for worshiping in natural settings whenever possible. I could and still do conduct my rituals in my garden or in the surrounding woods. However, it wasn't until I was leafing through my copy of *Cunningham's Encyclopedia of Magical Herbs* that a thought occurred to me.

"I can grow or locally source at least 60 percent of the plants he talks about in here," I realized.

That's what I have done since that time over two decades ago, both for myself and for others in my local Pagan community.

What Exactly Is an Herb?

Before getting into the meat of this book, I need to take a minute to talk about what I mean when I use the word *herb*.

A scientist will tell you that in taxonomy, the word *herb* refers to the aerial, above-ground portion of a plant. A botanist will tell you an herb is the leafy portion of a plant (usually annual or perennial) that is valued for its medicinal, cosmetic, or food qualities. The bark, seed, or nut of a plant is where spices come from.

Another way to say this would be leafy or tender parts of a plant are called herbs while non-leafy, dried bits of a plant are spices.

These definitions are a bit too rigid for magical purposes. For example, most witches don't consider acorns from an oak tree to be a spice. Plus, workers of magick get leaves for their various spells from an assortment of annuals, perennials, shrubs, and trees. In fact, people who work with plants for magickal purposes tend to follow the definition of herb as put forth by herbalists who practice medicine. For example, the American Botanical Council defines herbs as plant parts that are "used in various forms or preparations, valued for their therapeutic benefits, and sold as dietary supplements in the US marketplace. This includes trees, fungi, and marine substances."[1] Even *Merriam-Webster* will tell you that an herb is "a plant or plant part valued for its medicinal, savory, or aromatic qualities."[2] As I go through this book, I will say *herb* when I talk about roots, resins, flowers, nuts, bark, and leaves.

This is not meant to confuse anyone. The point of this book is to share information on Pagan practices, not educate anyone for a degree in botany.

Why Wildcraft?

Most of us probably think of popular herbs like frankincense, mandrake, or sandalwood when we think of herbs for magickal or religious purposes. These exotic plants have been used in traditional practices across ethnic groups for thousands of years. The problem is that they are hard or impossible to grow in most areas of the United States. What chance do you have of picking your own?

Consider, for instance, that most iconic of herbs, frankincense (*Boswellia sacra*) from the Boswellia tree. Depending on

---

1. "Taxonomy," American Botanical Council, last accessed June 16, 2020, https://abc.herbalgram.org/site/SPageServer/?pagename=Terminology.

2. *Merriam Webster*, s.v. "herb," accessed December 23, 2020, https://www.merriam-webster.com/dictionary/herb.

the variety of frankincense, the plant is native to Somalia, Yemen, Oman, Sudan, Ethiopia, India, or Pakistan. At one time, the tree was almost impossible to find in the United States. Today, a handful of reputable nurseries are growing the plant in Arizona and California.

However, as you can imagine, the tree needs hot, arid conditions in which to grow. The growing medium must be precisely mixed and feature lime gravel, perlite, or granite gravel. If you find seeds, the germination rate is abysmal—said to be anywhere from 1 percent to 16 percent. Growers seem to have more luck with sets but, again, cultivation can be spotty.

On top of that, assuming you can get the tree to grow, you will have to wait eight to ten years before it is old enough to produce resin. That is a long time to wait to perform a spell or an honoring.

Some of the more common herbs—things like lavender, lemongrass, and bloodroot—can be grown in most temperate areas but present problems. Lavender needs excellent drainage and full sun. Lemongrass grows well enough but requires prolonged warm temperatures that never drop below 20 degrees Fahrenheit. Bloodroot plants are hard to find and need a woodland setting to grow well. And what do you do if you don't have the space to grow your own herbs?

You could go to the kitchen. Check out your spice rack for useful dried herbs, such as basil for love, thyme for psychic powers, or poppy seed for fertility. Look about a little more in the kitchen and you'll probably find Asian tea for riches, garlic cloves for protection, and lemons for purification. These are all perfectly good herbs to use in the spells you might be planning.

This is all well and good, but the goal of the wildcrafting witch is to get in touch with the universe by collecting his or her own herbs. You don't need own a lush garden. You don't need to live next to a public garden. You can find herbs for any purpose just outside your door.

Look around. This is wildcrafted magick. You can find plenty of magickal herbs in your yard, your landscape, and even along the road to town. Mind you, I'm not talking about literally plying the highways in search of magickal herbs, although technically you could find a lot of what are called magickal herbs there. Unfortunately, most states and the federal government have laws against harvesting plants from the commercial roadside, mainly for safety reasons. Officials definitely don't want you raiding wildflower plantings from highway medians and rest stops!

In this case, when I talk about wildcrafting (especially for plants beyond your front or back yard), I mean the areas along your drive, the plants coming up in fields that you have legal access to, and plants that frequently border natural areas on your property. For example, within fifty feet of my back door, I have plantain for protection, honeysuckle for money and psychic powers, and cherry for love.

In select instances, I mean landscape plants with magickal attributes that are generally overlooked. Modern people don't often stop to think why their yards are landscaped with the plants that are there. For example, holly has always been considered a protective plant. Its spikey leaves not only keep thieves from the windows but also keep demons from the front door. Over time, people forgot or discounted the magickal aspects of holly and kept it for the practical value. Time moved on and Japanese hollies were introduced to Western markets. They had all the hardiness of native hollies without the spines. Spines on landscape plants aren't as important for security in the days of modern police forces and internet security companies. Plus, magickal or not, spiny hollies are a bear to prune—and at some point, they all need pruning.

As with a lot of things, we forget why we do the things we do. We do it just because—because our parents' house had hollies. Or the latest architectural magazine features landscape designs heavily reliant on hollies. Or hollies just randomly come back in vogue. Who knows? It doesn't matter. Hollies, like many plants, are landscape plants that can be harvested for their magickal properties.

This is the reason for this book. Come along and I will show you how to identify useful local plants and give you tips on collection and suggestions for processing those plants.

You'll also find a plant section in this book. I haven't tried to identify every single plant the average person is likely to see in the yard, just thirty-two to get you started. The plant identification section will tell you what the plant is, what planet governs it, what part of the plant to use, and what the uses are. Both common and Latin names are provided. Common names are much more colorful but can be confusing. What I call sweet Melisha, you might call sweet breath of spring. Either way, we are both talking about *Lonicera fragrantissima*, the shrub-form honeysuckle. Not to worry. You'll have illustrations to help you tell the difference.

In the plant section, I'll share with you my thirty-odd years of experience as a gardener as well as a magickal practitioner. In my journey, I have found that little anecdotes and interesting plant lore help me relate better to the plant. If nothing else, I can provide you with a bountiful supply of trivia to astound your friends.

I will also give you some suggestions for magickal projects specific to each plant that you might not have considered before.

I've tried not to get too technical when speaking about the horticultural information or too preachy when discussing the magickal information. Let's just pretend that we've come to the local public garden and coincidentally taken a rest on the same park bench for a time. Since we're here, why not pass the time sharing our mutual love of plants? Let's get the conversation started.

PART ONE

WILDCRAFTING

CHAPTER 1
Magick in a Modern World

Why are plants used for magick in the first place? You don't often see that question addressed in many magick books, old or new. The authors seem to proceed from the viewpoint that of course plants are magickal, so let's just get to talking about which plant to use for what purpose. But why would any rational modern reader want to believe that a plant could do anything beyond decorate their landscape or fill their dinner plate?

Our modern mindset doesn't give us much guidance. If you think of the "magick" of modern living, it mainly seems to revolve around machines and circuits—or more basically, metal and crystal. We get from one place to another in what people from 300 years ago would have considered magickal boxes (vehicles) propelled by magickal elixirs (petroleum). In fact, petroleum fuels our lives, at least for the foreseeable future. While some may point out that petroleum was at one time plant life, it hasn't been anywhere close to the plant kingdom in eons. Yes, we use corn for ethanol in some vehicles, but until somebody perfects the flying broom dusted with the right blends of herbs, we really can't say magick from plants physically transports us anywhere.

Today, we flip a switch or give a voice command to a mysterious black box that somehow carries out our bidding. "Siri (or Alexa or Cortana or whoever), turn down the lights and turn on the television." Bam! It happens. That is a magick that would truly confound our great-grandparents if they could only see us now. However, modern technology isn't what Pagans mean when they say "magick."

"Magick is the Science and Art of causing Change to happen in conformity with Will," if you believe Aleister Crowley.[3] Or if you prefer Dion Fortune, "Magick is the art of causing changes in consciousness in conformity with the will."[4] Donald Michael Kraig told us, "Magick is the science and art of causing change (in consciousness) to occur in conformity with will, using means not currently understood by traditional Western science."[5]

The definitions abound, many proposed by people far wiser than I. But you guessed it—I'm going to give you my two cents anyway.

If I had to put a concise definition to the word, I would say magick is the manipulation of natural forces with means and methods beyond those applied in the mundane world. It can be done with or without tools, with or without crystals, plants, or ceremonial robes. But all those items can help, as I will point out repeatedly throughout this book.

---

3. Aleister Crowley, *Magick in Theory and Practice: Part III of Book Four* (New York: Castle Books, 1929), xii.

4. Dion Fortune, "The Rationale of Magic," *London Forum* 60, no. 3 (September 1934), 175.

5. Donald Michael Kraig, *Modern Magick: Eleven Lessons in the High Magickal Arts* (St. Paul, MN: Llewellyn Publications, 1993), 10.

Uncovering the Historical Record

You may ask, who decided that burning a particular plant resin or brewing a certain plant leaf would somehow help us achieve peace in our life or put ducats in our pockets? Scholars suggest that the use of plants in magick developed hand-in-hand with the use of plants for medicine.[6] As humans experimented with plants to discover what fed and what healed them, they also developed community rituals to conduct as they consumed or used those plants. In time, the ritual and the plants became conflated. John Scarborough discusses this concept extensively in his essay "The Pharmacology of Sacred Plants, Herbs and Roots," one of ten essays concerning Greek traditions in *Magika Hiera: Ancient Greek Magic and Religion*.[7]

Using garlic, for example, during a communal ritual to heal someone of infection drove the bad spirits of infection away. If it worked on the bad spirits of infection (which people couldn't see), why wouldn't garlic work to drive bad spirits (which people couldn't see) of any sort away—be they spirits of envy, bad luck, or hard times?

Well, that is one way to look at it.

For others, the magick is inherent in the plant. Those who believe this rely largely on the doctrine of plant signatures. It is pretty well accepted in the Pagan community that twenty-first-century folks didn't come up with the notion of plant signatures.

---

6. Joshua J. Mark, "Ancient Egyptian Medical Texts," Ancient History Encyclopedia, February 21, 2017, https://www.ancient.eu/article/1015/ancient-egyptian-medical-texts/.

7. John Scarborough, "The Pharmacology of Sacred Plants, Herbs and Roots," in *Magika Hiera: Ancient Greek Magic and Religion*, ed. Christopher A. Faraone and Dirk Obbink (New York: Oxford University Press, 1997), 146.

Historical figures such as Galen, Dioscorides, and Paracelsus recorded the thinking of their times about plant signatures. Signatures are the attributes Pagans ascribe to plants. These ancient experts listed above believed the Divine put signs on plants to help people learn what plants to use for a particular goal.[8]

Actually, the medical community uses the term *signatures* too. Not traditional doctors, at least not anymore, but homeopathic caregivers do talk about signatures to mean "like with like." In this case, it means stinging nettle (*Urtica doicia*) can help alleviate the pain of stinging insects, for example, because the plant is covered with tiny, hairy stingers that burn like the devil when you touch them. The spotted leaves of lungwort (*Pulmonaria officinalis*) looked to healers of old like lung tissue. It grows in damp places. It made sense to them that the plant could be useful in treating ailments of the lungs.

Just to clarify here, there had to have been a lot of trial and error in this approach. Carolina horsenettle (*Solanum carolinense*) has stinging needles too. Nobody is suggesting you should brew a wash of horsenettle tea to soothe your mosquito bites. In fact, please don't use this plant medicinally at all. It has some limited medical benefits but only when used under the direction of a trained herbalist. This is especially true of *Atropa belladonna,* or deadly nightshade, a plant in the Solanaceae family. In fact, don't ingest any leafy material from a plant in this family. The harvest is okay for the most part (i.e., tomatoes and potatoes). At best some of the foliage from the plants in this family can make you seriously ill; at worst a few can make you seriously dead.

8. Bradley C. Bennet, "Doctrine of Signatures: An Explanation of Medicinal Plant Discovery or Dissemination of Knowledge?" *Economic Botany* 61, no. 3 (2007): 246, https://www.jstor.org/stable/4257221?seq=1.

Pagans use a similar approach to the guidelines of signatures to tell us what plant to use in which spell or meditation. The idea is that each plant has a particular energy. If you match the plant energy to your purpose in doing a meditation or spell, the chance of success is improved. In magick, plants are typically masculine or feminine in nature. This means they have the characteristics or properties typically associated with the genders. For example, masculine plants have defense mechanisms like thistles or fiery constituents like radishes. Feminine plants are soft, frequently with large, showy flowers. Their actions are gentler in magick or in the body.

Plants can be hot, cold, wet, or dry. They are assigned to or governed by one of seven (or nine, depending on your outlook) heavenly bodies. People assigned these characteristics based on where a plant grew, what it looked like, and what effect it had on the humans and animals that came in contact with the plant.

If you eat a peppercorn, your body reacts by becoming warm. That must mean the plant contains fire—not literally but in essence. Fire purifies. It burns away most things it touches and makes animals and people run away when it is out of control, which in the ancient world happened with unfortunate frequency. Fire is a good thing, if used with caution. It protects. Add all this up and you might decide that peppercorns contain the essence of the masculine protector who also exorcises bad things from your presence. Because it is aggressive in its heat, you might be inclined to assign this plant to Mars, that fiery red celestial body named after the Roman god of war. Different religious traditions have different names for their gods and goddesses of ferocity and war, so your god may vary. But the ancient traditions that many American Pagans seem to gravitate toward are based on European deities, so I'll continue in this vein. No offense intended.

This is just one example. Some researchers will say the doctrine of signatures begins in the Middle Ages with Jacob Boehme (1575–1624 CE). One of the earliest books on the subject, *The Signature of All Things*, was written in 1621 by Boehme, a Christian mystic. Boehme does get credit for promoting the concept. If you can find a copy of it, you will see it is very heavy on references to alchemy and Biblical allusions. Provided you can get past the Lutheran influences, you will recognize quite a bit of what Pagans tend to accept as true about plants. It should be noted that Boehme's approach to medicine, religion, and his church were very controversial, and he was regularly hauled up before the religious authorities of the time and threatened with excommunication for this and other books he wrote.

Boehme was influenced by Paracelsus (1495–1541), who seems to have had better luck in promoting the notion of signatures. So did William Cole (1626–1662 CE), who wrote a very successful book titled *The Art of Simpling, or an Introduction to the Knowledge and Gathering of Plants.*

The doctrine of signatures goes back much further than the Middle Ages. You don't have to read very far in Maud Grieve's *A Modern Herbal,* to see references to plant signatures from authorities such as Cornelius Agrippa (1486–1534 CE), Chaucer (1343–1400 CE), Galen (131–201 CE), and Dioscorides (c. 40–c. 90 CE). Dioscorides's knowledge seems to have been based, at least in part, on that of Hippocrates (460–377 BCE) and practitioners who lived hundreds of years before him. While Paracelsus is generally accepted as one of the first to write down the concept that plants are marked in nature according to their benefit to mankind, it is clear many herbalists and philosopher-scientists prior to him understood this idea.

Bringing the Past into the Future

Unless a plant is incorporated into Western traditions from other cultures, no reputable source that I know of is coming up with any new classifications for magickal plants. I frequently see websites and Facebook entries that offer suggestions on how to use plants that make me sit back and shake my head. Where did that author get his or her information? Is this personal experience talking? I'm not trying to judge anyone's personal spiritual progress. Still, if I see someone suggesting the way to ease a broken heart is with a spell that is based on chili pepper as the main ingredient, red flags start to go up. Maybe the author has personal experience with "burning away the pain" using a fiery herb. The suggestion still gives me pause. I would suggest in magick, as in anything in life, consider the source, keep an open but critical mind and question where the information is coming from before you invest your time.

If we aren't going to take advice from just any tinker we come across on the internet, who can we trust? Fortunately, we have some time-tested experts we can rely on who left us scraps of papyrus and early manuscripts based on their own knowledge. Be warned. A few of those folks were quacks and charlatans too. For example, *The Fourth Book of Occult Philosophy* was promoted as having been written by Agrippa, who was the author and Christian practitioner who published *The Three Books of Occult Philosophy*. However, the book was not written by Agrippa, as has been pointed out over the years by various experts, including nineteenth-century British occult author and mystic A. E. Waite. Waite wrote that the authorship of the fourth book was in dispute even at the time of its publication in 1559, thirty years after Agrippa's death.[9] It is mostly a rehash of information from Agrippa's *Three Books of Occult Philosophy*. It just goes to show, plagiarism was alive and well even in the early days.

I have built a basic list of what I consider to be reliable resources from which to get background information on magickal uses for plants. Some of these were not written from a magickal perspective. The authors were collecting all the information they could find in order to preserve a cultural heritage before it was lost. In other cases, the goal was to understand the ways in which ancestors used plants for healing. The author would frequently turn up his or her academic nose as he or she recounted how people used herbs to appease fairies, for example. Fortunately for us, they tried to record the information any way. These resources are listed in a bibliography at the end of this book.

For plants from other cultures, the standard practice is to either wholly adopt what their old legends tell us or make a correlation with our own Western traditions.

Why does this matter for us? What has it all got to do with the purpose of this book? On the one hand, I am telling you to learn to use what might be considered nontraditional plants. On the other hand, I am insisting that you research old resources and mages who might not have known about the plants you see in your landscape.

Well, if you are a stickler for tradition, it could mean a lot. I would maintain that you can and should use plant material in your immediate area. Others would say to let the ancients from cultures across the globe be our guides. If they say use rose-

---

9. Arthur Edward Waite, *The Book of Black Magic* (Boston: Weiser Books, 2002), 74.

mary (*Salvia rosmarinus,* syn. *Rosmarinus officinalis*) for cleansing, then white sage (*Salvia apiana*), a plant that is native to the Americas, just won't do. Sticklers would argue that a spell will only work if you use precisely the materials that are called for in an old grimoire.

This is understandable. Generally, a lot of credence is assigned to a practice if it can be traced back in a continuous line to an ancient authority or population. If Ptolemy said it, it must be so, for example. If the item or author in question is exotic to us, so much the better. Garden club speakers in my area used to have a saying in the gardening lecture circuit: an "expert" was anyone with a slide projector and a willingness to travel over fifty miles to give a presentation. What is that old Christian saying? "A prophet is not without honor except in his own town, among his relatives and in his own home."[10] If that expert voice is coming from several centuries back and has withstood the test of time, so much the better. You can't get much further from home than a thousand or more years ago and dead.

For those who are hardcore in their magickal persuasion, when the banishing spell calls for asafetida (*Ferula assa-foetida*), he or she might not be interested in substituting pokeroot (*Phytolacca americana*). Asafetida, or devil's dung, is grown in the area now called Afghanistan as well as other places in the Middle East and would have been well known to the ancient practitioners. Its signatures or characteristics were identified so long ago we will probably never know for sure who first officially described and recommended them.

Pokeroot would have been alien to the cultures in the Middle East before the Common Era or in Europe in the Middle Ages.

---

10. Mark 6:4, New International Version.

Europeans would have learned about poke from native populations in North, Central, and South America. The plant has been in use, in all likelihood, as long as asafetida. We just don't have the American equivalent of a Dioscorides to standardize its use.

Both asafetida and pokeweed do a fine job in banishing or hexing spells. The problem is I have a hard time finding asafetida and have yet to find anyone who will sell me seeds or sets to grow my own. On the other hand, I can find pokeroot any day of the year within a hundred yards of my house. I could order asafetida online, but like most of my generation, whenever I want it (whatever it is), I want it now! Even Amazon's next-day delivery isn't soon enough if the moon is in the right phase for my spell tonight.

Plus, I want to connect with my herbs personally by collecting and processing my own. The idea of using something within my reach suits my needs. It may not suit the hardcore traditionalist.

Then there is the question of plant identification. Let's say I want a wand made of oak (*Quercus*). Oak is a fine sturdy wood revered, researchers like J. A. MacCulloch say, by Druids of Europe.[11] I could cut material for my wand from an oak found on the North American continent at the right time, cure it in the oldest of traditions, carve it, and dedicate it with precise care and still not be entirely true to the Druids of old. That's because I would likely be using white oak (*Quercus alba*) and not English oak (*Q. robur*) or Sessile oak (*Q. petraea*), often found in England, France, or Germany, where early Druids practiced.

Is this a problem? Strictly speaking, it is if one wants to "follow the letter of the law." When the task calls for a particular

---

11. J. A. MacCulloch, *The Religion of the Ancient Celts* (Edinburgh, UK: T&T Clark, 1911), 198.

plant, one should use only the plants called for by the practitioners of old—no substitutions. I don't think we need to be so rigid. White oaks, just like live oaks, water oaks, burr oaks, and so on, are all in the oak family. They all possess the characteristics of their European cousins, including strength, protection, healing powers, luck, and fertility. I can use white oak in magick without any thought that it will somehow lessen the potency of the magick.

Finally, people tend to think of the plant kingdom as static. It isn't. Plants evolve. They change. A good example is the wild violet (*Viola*). Without a doubt, Europeans brought *Viola odorata* to the New World. It escaped into the wild and comingled with the native *V. arvensis*, *V. sororia*, and on and on. In fact, there seems to be no North American cousin in the viola family that hasn't comingled at some point. There is a reason why the herbalists of old attributed this plant to Venus even without the benefit of genetic testing. It's a randy little critter that gets along with everybody in its family tree! It's so intermingled that botanists tell us you need a degree and a lab to get the identification right.

All the violas we can find growing in our lawns still have the characteristics of the original plant albeit with some variations that the layperson would never be able to identify by casual observation. Is it the exact same plant today that Agrippa spoke of when he ascribed this "flower of innocence" to Venus?[12] I don't know. I doubt it. But I am comfortable with the thought that all the violets in my yard still have the characteristics of "sweet, unctuous, and delectable."[13]

---

12. Henry Cornelius Agrippa, *Three Books of Occult Philosophy*, trans. James Freake, ed. Donald Tyson (St. Paul, MN: Llewellyn Publications, 2004), 91.

13. Agrippa, *Three Books of Occult Philosophy*, 91.

Why This Works

Before leaving this chapter, let's consider one more stand on plants. I have read any number of authors or experts and attended more than one class where a teacher said plants aren't necessary for a spell or ritual. In fact, they will say nothing is necessary for magickal work except your intent.

Don't have a wand? Your finger will do. Don't have a consecrated candle? Use the birthday candle in the back of the kitchen utility drawer. Don't have flax for that beauty spell? Use rosemary or grass or the dust bunny from under the sofa. Nothing matters but your intent, or more specifically, the power of your intent. Technically, these folks are right.

Summon up your personal energy in the middle of a busy freeway at high noon with no accoutrements and you should be able to complete your spell with the same success as when you work it in the right hour, in a ritual robe, with all your consecrated tools and herbs in the privacy of a sacred, secret circle. My mother used to tell me the same thing about my powers of concentration when my brothers were yelling bloody murder and I was trying to complete a homework assignment. She was right, of course. But that doesn't mean that having a quiet setting and all the right tools wouldn't have made completing my homework assignment a lot easier.

I also wonder when I hear instructors say herbs aren't necessary for spells if they really think their students' powers of concentration and intent are that strong or if they believe saying it makes it so. As I understand it, it takes years of study and meditation to develop the skills to stand naked in the world and summon the kind of energy needed for any magickal task. What was the longest period of time that you devoted to meditation to firmly establish your contact to the Divine? Can you focus your attention strongly enough to call the wind? Do you routinely whip out spells that achieve the results you ask for with certainty?

I did landscape work for a number of years. I also taught landscape maintenance classes. I gave my students guidelines on when, where, and what to plant. I also talked with my students about what happens when you decide not to follow the guidelines. Surprisingly, stuff still grows. Plant grass seed on a north slope without irrigation in the middle of July in the southern half of the United States, and you might actually get a good stand of grass. Chances are you won't, but it could happen.

I look at my herbs the same way. I try to devote time to meditation. I continue to work on my connection to the universe. Sometimes I'm not as regimented as I should be. I have observed that my meditations and spells aren't as successful if I don't keep up the work on my personal spiritual growth. By the same token, I've done everything right (herbs and all) and had spells fail miserably.

I don't believe any Harry or Brunhilda can go to an herb cabinet, blend a potion according to recipe, and *poof!* the spell is a success. It takes time to develop the skills in energy raising, energy focusing, and power of intent to accomplish the work. Herbs, like ritual tools, help us focus intent.

I cannot stress this strongly enough.

The same is true when you work with plants for magick. You have to experience the life cycle of the plant. Touch the plant. Smell the plant. If it is safe to consume, taste the plant. When the blend is right, the tactile interaction with plants can unlock the recesses of the mind, bringing the proper feelings into play that help to build the necessary energy for a spell. Just experiencing the texture of the plant material can help create the right atmosphere. How could anyone feel the delicate, soft texture of a rose petal and not think of a gentle caress? And this doesn't even begin to address the metaphysical properties of plants.

Which brings us back to wildcrafted magick. Interacting with nature, gathering your herbs, processing and storing them; it all allows you to focus on your magickal work. This work will involve you deeply with whatever project you are working on. This is another way to grow magickly.

Think of making this commitment to harvest your own herbs in the same way you think about cooking. You can feed yourself or your family with prepared meals from the grocery freezer. That doesn't make you lazy or uncaring. It makes you a busy person who doesn't prioritize cooking.

When you want to do something special for yourself or family, you may purchase the ingredients for the same menu items that came in that frozen meal and actually breakout the pots and pans. If you really want to make a commitment, you might grow your own produce or visit a local pick-your-own farm for fresh vegetables and fruit. You will clean them and process them yourself, all the while thinking in the back of your mind of the love you have for yourself and your family or friends.

Once you are done, whether you eat the end result immediately or put it up for future use, you have a sense of involvement that doesn't come from opening a can or defrosting a prepackaged meal. Nothing beats the bragging rights of saying, when you bring those vegetables to the table, "I grew these myself" or "I got these from the farm down the road and put them up just for this occasion."

You put your personal energy into those plants, whether you are a witch or not. Many modern practitioners tell us they meditate on positive energy when they cook, hoping to bring that much more love and health to those they care for. You will be doing the same thing when you harvest and process some of your own magickal herbs from around your home.

Don't throw out your traditional herbs. Don't stop supporting your local New Age shop. I would never want to be without my dragon's blood or myrrh or any of the other things I rely on local vendors to supply. But I don't want to limit myself either. Hopefully, you agree. If you're still with me, let's get started.

Chapter 2

Ground Rules before You Harvest

First, I must set up some ground rules. How do we know which plant to harvest? Where are we going to get our plants? How do we help ourselves without harming the local environment? Do we gather willy-nilly in a Captain Jack Sparrow "Take what you can, give nothing back" approach, or do we focus our search? If so, how do we do that? Where do we find learning resources beyond what are provided here? The answers to these questions will aid you as you begin your wildcrafting journey.

When I first conceived of the idea to write this book, the economy was not on solid ground. My friends and I were frequently strapped for money. As I mentioned before, you don't have to have herbs to do a ritual or a spell, but using them does enhance the energy and the experience. I am reasonably sure that while the Divine is not so petty as to shun an applicant who doesn't have the money for sandalwood incense to perform an honoring, that doesn't mean having it isn't appreciated.

In our cash-strapped state, several of us had taken to substituting locally available herbs when possible. It was a short step from this action to the realization, "Hey, everybody can do this." Having taught gardening classes, my next realization was, "Yes, they can, but only with a little instruction on what to gather."

Learning the Plants' Names

Unless you have been active in landscaping and gardening, you may need help identifying the plant in the wild beyond the visual aids in this book. Your local cooperative extension office is a good place to start. This state-funded and federally funded organization is in business to help homeowners properly grow shrubs, trees, flowers, grass, veggies, and herbs. They will have plenty of information, some of it with good color pictures, that you can take with you. Also, watch for local classes on home landscaping.

This resource plays to another reason why I have written this book. I assume everyone wants to save money. Plus, a good witch, in my opinion, is a financially savvy witch. The materials available through state extension services are typically provided free or at very low cost. Cooperative extensions also helps homeowners identify weeds. However, what most homeowners call weeds, Pagans call magickal resources!

The internet can be your friend, if you have an idea of what you are looking for. In my experience, having both the Latin name and the common name for the plant you are interested in helps.

For the longest time, I resisted learning the scientific names of the plants I was interested in. It seemed so snobbish to go around talking about my desire to own an *Oxydendrum arboreum* when I could simply say I wanted a sourwood tree. It turns out, a good reason exists for learning those pesky Latin terms. Otherwise, a blanket search for poplar, for example, could net you plenty of

pictures of aspen (*Populus tremuloides*) instead of the tulip poplar (*Liriodendron tulipifera*) you were interested in.

As you look through the list of plants in chapter 6, you will
see that I have included the Latin names for the entries. I will
talk in a little greater detail about plant nomenclature in that
chapter. For now, you should know the system of naming plants
was developed by Carl Linnaeus and is called binomial nonmen-
clature. For those unfamiliar with the way plants get their Latin
names, the first word in the name is the plant genus and is capitalized. The second word is the species. It helps tell us specifically
which plant in the genus is being discussed. When the discussion
turns to more than one type of plant in the genus, the first name
is abbreviated to just the capitalized first letter, followed by the
species name. Sometimes the species name will be followed by a
varietal or cultivar name.

For example, the first plant I talk about in chapter 6 is box-
wood, or *Buxus*. Specifically, I talk about the American boxwood,
Buxus sempervirens, and the English boxwood, *B. sempervirens*
'Suffruticosa'.

Don't get hung up on this. I hope you will continue to explore
the plants around your home after you read this book. The Latin
names will help you with future research. Trust me. The Divine
doesn't care if you memorize the Latin names of the plants you
use in your ritual. When you gather honeysuckle, the plant is not
going to be offended if you fail to call it *Lonicera japonica* (the vining honeysuckle) or *L. fragrantissima* (the winter honeysuckle).

Where to Find Plants

My friends and I gather plant material from our own yards. My
urban friends are a bit more challenged and limited in what is
available. I'm not ashamed to rat them out and say more than one

or two have picked plant material from public spaces or areas that did not belong to them.

I think there is a tendency among the general public to think of public spaces as being fair game for everyone. But keep in mind in our Western society, all property "belongs" to somebody. You may believe in your heart that no one can own a piece of Mother Earth. Trust me, the local authorities will tend to disagree with you.

Access to easements along public roads belongs to area governments. The property along the railroad tracks belongs to some railroad company. If you don't think the railroad companies are adamant about their property rights, you've never been to a zoning hearing. Even the vacant lot that seems to be abandoned belongs to somebody. While no one is likely to complain if you gather a dandelion from the crack in the sidewalk, property owners of all sorts will probably get upset if you show up with a pair of pruners and start lopping branches off a mimosa tree on that open lot.

And don't get me started on public parks and arboretums. I have actually heard people express the sentiment, "My tax dollars paid for this, so it's okay if I pull up a plant or break off a branch and take it home with me." I've been on garden trips to facilities owned by a private estate and heard people say, "They've got so much money that they can always buy more plants. So what if I take a piece and try to root it in my own garden?"

Your tax dollars may have contributed to the construction of that public arboretum but, if that is the case, so did mine. I don't appreciate people vandalizing property I helped pay for. And if you believe it's okay for you to take from a private owner, that mindset only works, in my opinion, if you are also okay with a stranger wandering into your yard and helping himself to plants because his economic condition is worse than yours.

More importantly, ripping and tearing at plants is very disrespectful to the plant and to the local environment generally. I'll talk a little later about how to gather plant material properly. For now, let's just state emphatically I do not endorse snatching plant material from public or private plant collections.

Next, did you realize that a utility easement belongs to a private property owner? Many folks think these areas are abandoned or owned by an absentee utility company that only shows up once a year for maintenance. Utility companies do own some land outright but, in the majority of cases, this is not true. For the public good and in exchange for a promise to do property maintenance, private property owners give utilities permission to access transmission lines that run across their property. That permission does not extend to the community at large.

I am blessed to live in the middle of roughly 100 acres of woods with adjacent fields. I have permission to gather plant material from the utility easement beside my house. Be certain you do too.

Protecting the Local Environment

You must remember—for you, herbs are a tool to supplement magick. For the area wildlife, herbs and plants are food and shelter. The plant you hope to gather has a part to play in the local ecosystem. In some cases, it may have a symbiotic relationship with another plant, bacteria, or fungus in that area. The plant you want may need that relationship to survive, but the bacteria or fungus also needs the plant. Taking the plant might mean more than eliminating one plant—it could mean wiping out associated life.

Always bear in mind. You have no right to wipe out an entire colony of running cedar (*Diphasiastrum digitatum*), for example, and deprive the local wildlife of the coverage and fodder they may need. Be certain that you collect no more than what you need. A general rule of thumb is to take no more than one-third of the available material.

This might be a good point to stop and point out that I am talking about common plants that can be gathered for your purposes, not endangered, threatened, or protected species. For example, you may find in your magickal resource books a plant commonly called Adam and Eve root (*Aplectrum hyemale*). It is also known as putty root. The plant is found in most of the eastern half of the United States. If you are lucky, you might see this native orchid in your walks through undisturbed wooded areas.

In magick, this plant is used to attract or keep a lover. The user is supposed to dig up and dry the two very distinctive tubers that support the plant. These are carried in a gris-gris or mojo bag to have an effect.

But check before you dig. In most states where it is found, Adam and Eve root is listed as a special concern plant. In other states, it is listed as threatened. That means the plant population is in danger of being lost due to shrinking habitat.

Adam and Eve root is an example of a plant with a wide range. Every state has pockets of special plants that are protected against harvest. In my area, a pretty wildflower called Schweinitz's sunflower (*Helianthus schweinitzii*) is found in select areas. To the untrained eye, it looks a lot like a more common cousin, the swamp sunflower (*H. angustifolius*).

Pagans from all traditions can use some sunflower energy in their lives from time to time. For ritual purposes, sunflower is used to honor Sol, Magec, Etain, and Wi, among other solar deities, and to raise solar attributes of fire, fertility, and protection. But don't do that with Schweinitz's sunflowers. These are the rarest native sunflowers in the United States. They only grow in Piedmont North Carolina and two adjacent counties in South Carolina.

A good rule of thumb to remember is what you *can* gather and what you *should* gather are two different things. Don't contribute to the decline of the native plant populations in your area by collecting protected plants. Do your research before you decide to dig. As I said earlier, plants in the same genus have the same attributes. An oak (*Quercus alba*) is an oak (*Q. robur*) is an oak (*Q. petraea*), as it were. If your spell calls for a plant that is on the endangered list, find a substitute in the same plant genus.

The list of endangered and threatened plants changes frequently. Some plants come off the list; others go on it. Sadly, some plants become extinct. Another complicating factor is that a plant might be listed as endangered in one state but not in another. Because the list varies, the internet is the best resource to find out if a plant is safe to harvest in your area.

I recommend using the database provided by the US Department of Agriculture Natural Resources Conservation Service at https://plants.usda.gov/threat.html. Your tax dollars go to maintaining a pretty accurate list here of endangered plants by region and state. On the rare occasion that the responsibility for managing the list moves to a different agency, the federal government generally does a good job of redirecting you to the new site.

Another federal resource is the US Fish and Wildlife Service at https://www.fws.gov/endangered/. Here, you can research plants by state and county.

I can find a list of endangered plants in North Carolina at the state cooperative extension service. That may or may not be true for your state but it's a good place to start your search, if you prefer looking for resources closer to home. Many nonprofit organizations work to maintain their own lists. However, these organizations aren't always up to date. Unfortunately, depending on the amount of donations received, they may or may not stay active. Whatever resource you use, make sure to check a plant's status before you harvest.

Plant Parts

Once you know what plant you need, the next step is to understand what part of the plant is required. Why would a responsible witch pull up an entire plant if they only needed the leaves or the flower? The answer is they wouldn't do that.

The best books tell you which plant to use and what part of that plant is most effective. For example, yellow dock (*Rumex crispus*) is used for prosperity (specifically in money spells or to attract business), but what part of the yellow dock? It's the seeds. In most cases, seeds of various plants are the part used to attract prosperity.

You'll find that the roots of plants are frequently used for dark purposes. By "dark," I don't mean evil. I mean banishing or breaking hexes. Good examples of this would be poke or mayapple (*Podophyllum peltatum*) root. Roots are also beneficial in spells that help you ground or stabilize a situation. They are key to connecting with the chthonic deities as well. Think Hecate, Osiris, and many more.

Flowers are often used for love and companionship. The color of the flower will frequently be important to the nature of that love. Leaves or bark cover a lot of the other needs. These aren't hard and fast rules—for example, mandrake roots can be used in money spells as well as protection spells—but this will give you some general guidelines.

Personal Safety

An important consideration for personal safety is pollution. Pollution is fairly obvious in terms of trash that clutters the roadside or piles up in our homes. It is bad enough when it clogs landfills, rotting and oozing into our groundwater. But pollution is also billowing clouds spewing from a smokestack or fumes from the car exhaust. Sadly, these contributors and others cause more than lung irritation. Pollutants settle on leaves. They seep into the ground with each rainfall. Plants take up certain chemicals.

The herbs that I gather from the wild will be used in incense or in gris-gris bags. I do not intend to eat them or smoke them or drink an infusion from them. I grow my own herbs for those purposes. When gathering plants away from your home, your control, you will have no idea what has been applied to or absorbed by the plant. Do not ingest them in any form.

Take into consideration the potential for allergies. You might be allergic to mulberries. You will definitely have a reaction to poison ivy. I say again, don't ingest any of the plants you gather if you don't personally know how you will react to that plant or the life history of that plant.

Matching Plants to Your Intent

We're still not quite ready to head outside yet. Let's think about what we will be gathering our plants for. There are three basic needs that I've noticed most people seem to be interested in: love, protection, and prosperity.

I can break that down a little further. There is love of family, friendship, and the sexual love of a companion. To go a little further, you may be looking for a lustful companion, a snuggle-bunny companion, or a platonic companion.

Under protection, you can set up wards or boundaries—a kind of passive protection. Or you can do a more active protection spell like a banishing. The most active would be either breaking or establishing a hex. Or you may just want to build your courage and strength to face a particular situation.

Prosperity has many aspects as well. Most often people think simply in terms of "more money." But the more specific we make our goals, the easier it can be to achieve them. Maybe you need a quick windfall of cash. You can certainly work on that, but in my experience, the universe doesn't seem to understand paper money. Instead of working to win the lottery or to find a bag of money on the side of the road, broaden your outlook.

You can get more money by getting a better job or a promotion at an existing job. Prosperity can mean something more tangible, like you need a better means of transportation than your current old rust bucket. Or maybe you would like the universe to align in such a way that you can afford to further your education. Frankly, you should also consider if the problem you're having with money isn't that you don't have enough. It might be that you don't have the self-control to properly manage what you have. In other words, instead of looking for clover for prosperity, maybe you should be looking for mimosa for divine consultation.

I should also mention that spirituality is something that many of us strive for, even if it may not also be the first item on our wish list. You might be looking for herbs that are helpful in meditation or personal development. These are also readily available just outside your door.

Before you harvest, take some time to think about what you need, either immediately or in the long term. It's okay to gather more than what you need for one spell as long as you have a true intention to make use of the material in a timely manner.

Don't gather something just to say you have it. That's not being a responsible steward of your local environment. I'll talk in a later chapter about how to preserve your harvest. However, most herbs should be used in roughly one year from gathering. After that, what remains should be returned to nature. At that time you can reassess your needs to determine if you really want to go out to gather more.

Shadow Magick

While I am talking about needs, I think I should discuss the dark side of magick. I realize the topic of dark versus light magick is a contentious one. You might ask why I would even include information on dark magick. Personally, I believe we are all adults, and this is a subjective topic. I have been in situations where someone needed to be bound because of their destructive behavior. It wasn't enough to project love at that person. They were not receptive to love. It was not enough to ward myself. I tend to want to be proactive when danger is present. If the copperhead snake is coiled in front of me and I can't avoid it, I need to do something proactive to ensure it doesn't bite me. I can't just blow kisses at it.

Technically, that means taking a dark approach to magick. Will it come back to me? Possibly. Whether you believe in the law of three or in Newtonian laws of physics, you might say the negative energy will definitely rebound to me. This brings up the big C word in magick. There are consequences to everything you do.

I have been approached by people who have no problem with using dark magick or the left-hand path to get rid of a romantic rival or to complicate the life of a coworker—as long they are not the ones actually doing the work. They are willing to pay someone to do that for them. Think of it as an escape clause, a kind of plausible deniability. This is the coward's way out. I also believe, if you are putting that kind of negative energy out into the world, that it doesn't matter whether you do the work or have someone else do it for you. The universe isn't stupid. It will come back to you.

I highly recommend that you don't do negative magick for someone else. I won't tell you not to use darker means to fix a problem for yourself if you have exhausted all other means. There used to be a saying around where I grew up: "Ya weighs the odds and takes yer chances" (in the local vernacular). I'm a big girl. You can make up your own mind.

Timing

Next, keeping in mind that there is a time for everything, there is a time to gather your herbs. Generally, spells done for positive outcomes—such as prosperity and love—are done during the waxing moon. Spells for banishing problems or breaking bad habits are done in the waning moon. Frankly, spells that are done to bind or hex are done in the waning or dark moon. It makes sense that you should gather your herbs at the right phase of the moon as well. In chapter 3, I'll talk in more detail about some of the thoughts and theories about harvesting by moon phases and heavenly bodies.

But here's a consideration. What happens if your need is more pressing and you can't wait two weeks for the moon to cycle or even a few days for the right day to come along? You can still gather your herbs. Do your spell with as much energy and focus as you normally would. You should be all right. It's just that, as with any project, you want as many things going in your favor as possible. That's why I stress gathering herbs within the proper time frame.

Finally, here's another interesting question. Periodically, nature will gift you with something. Maybe it's something you need in your life. Maybe she's just feeling froggy and decided to put something in your path to see what you would do with it. If I find some lovely oak moss cast in my path on a Sunday, do I have to wait until Monday to pick it up? (Oak moss is a moon herb and Monday is the moon's day.) If you wait until Monday, go back to fetch the oak moss and it is gone, does that mean you weren't meant to have it? Or does that mean that Mother Goddess or Father God is just jerking you around a bit?

This could devolve into one of those discussions about how many angels can dance on the head of a pin. Fallen material is fair game any day of the week in my opinion. If you need it, gather it. Then invest it with the proper energy. If not, just appreciate nature's bounty and leave it for someone else.

CHAPTER 3

Heavenly Bodies and Their Impact on Plants

Before you make the first cut, I want to talk a little more about planetary rulership, the significance of the moon in our work and how to use this information for more successful herbal combinations. As mentioned before, having as many factors going in your favor as possible helps to ensure you receive the best possible outcome when working magick. To be most precise, this means harvesting a plant on the right day when the proper planet is in the right zodiac sign in the sky. On the most basic level, that means harvesting when the moon is in the right phase for the work you are doing—increasing for positive magick, decreasing for baneful magick.

How Planets Influence Plants

When resources say this planet or that rules a plant, what is meant by this? It means that plants under the rulership of a particular planet share similar characteristics. Many of these can be found in any good book on alchemy. That said, I can sum up the list like this:

Sun: Vigor, vitality; plants that look like the sun or that generate a feeling of warmth

Moon: Governing most plants for divination or that have plant parts shaped like the moon; plants that affect sleep

Mercury: Fine-textured plants; plants that grow fast; plants that affect speech and communication

Venus: Most sweet-smelling flowers; plants for relationships; plants that produce red fruit; plants that have a fuzzy texture

Mars: Plants with spines or thorns; plants that are protective in a proactive sense; spicy plants, particularly those that generate a sensation of heat when eaten

Jupiter: Aromatic plants; big plants; plants for prosperity and abundance; most yellow plants, particulary those that stimulate bile production

Saturn: Slow-growing plants; plants that make connections to the underworld; plants that like cool, dry, shaded places; plants that affect mood and age

How do planets influence plants? In magickal thinking, there is a macrocosm and a microcosm. Everything beyond the realm of the mundane here on Earth is the macrocosm. Everything on Earth is a microcosm. The macrocosm sets the agenda. The microcosm reflects the agenda. The microcosm is a subset of the macrocosm.

Pythagoras is credited with formally detailing this philosophy. He applied his theory about the macrocosm and microcosm from the universe on a grand scale all the way down to the individual—as in the individual is a microcosm of the societal macrocosm.[14]

Applying it to magick, if you know the characteristics of the larger heavenly bodies, you can look around to see what plants reflect those characteristics. For example, Mars, the fiery god of war, and his planet generate heat—not radiant solar heat but heat that comes from action. Sometimes that is action without thought, but it is still action in a fierce, no-holds-barred kind of way. The god of war approaches with weapons of offense to pierce the flesh. He is a type A personality, writ large.

Once you know which plants fit the category of Mars, you can bring those qualities into your life as needed. Of course, you might try asking Mars directly to help you. According to the Greeks, that didn't always work. Greek deities could be fickle in their dealings with humans. They might show up; they might not. If they did show up, they might not help you in the way you asked. They definitely wanted to be recognized with rituals and honorings. They just weren't the most responsive overseers.

That's okay. In magick, you can still get the results you want by putting Mars plants to work for you. Think that is an absurd line of thought? It is still done today. Depending on the impression one wants to make, one takes on the "correspondences" appropriate to one's needs. One dresses up for corporate functions with special clothing, the right perfume or cologne and correct speech. Using modern correspondences, this person takes on the associations of Jupiter—big, bold, and in charge. He or she affects an appearance of affluence in the hopes of manifesting that in

---

14. W. K. C. Guthrie, *The Greek Philosophers from Thales to Aristotle* (New York: Harper Perennial, 1975), 37.

real life. If one does it well enough, it works. The same is true of magick.

Moon Sign versus Day Correspondences

Now let's talk about the moon and planetary correspondence. This may get a little complicated. I have said that whenever possible, you should gather plants at a time when the planetary ruler is most prominent. At its heart, this relies on correspondences that were codified millinia ago in Babylonia and Eygpt. These spread to Greece and Rome. The knowledge was written down, hidden in the Dark Ages, rediscovered in the Middle Ages, and discounted in the Industrial Age. I won't rehash the history here but will simply try to explain some of the reasoning behind both approaches.

By the Moon

For witchcraft, the best time to gather plants is when the moon is in the right phase and in the sign that governs the plant. Remember, each zodiac sign is governed by a particular planet. The moon can move into a sign at any point of the day. Generally, it takes the moon two and a half days to completely move through the sign.

When the moon is between signs, it is said to be void of course. This is not a good time to pick herbs or do magick. The energy is out of control. It's like a car careening down the road with no driver.

Using the moon to help determine when to do stuff is as old as humankind. All farmers' almanacs provide charts of the moon's progress through the signs. That's not to say that all farmers are Pagans. When farmers and gardeners use the moon to determine when to plant, prune, and harvest crops, they are following a centuries-old tradition of beliefs. According to this system, each different type of plant will do best when managed in the correct moon phase and when the moon is in the right astrological sign. If you would like to learn more about the history and rationale behind this topic, a great little book that has been in publication since 1993 is *Raising with the Moon* by authors Jack R. Pyle and Taylor Reese.

By the Planets

Plant material can also be gathered on the appropriate day or in the appropriate hour. This is based on the Chaldean system of ordering the hours and the days. Each day was assigned to a planet from the slowest, Saturn, to the fastest, the moon. In order these would be Saturn, Jupiter, Mars, the sun, Venus, Mercury, and the moon. Only those celestial bodies that could be seen by the naked eye were used to develop this practice. People born before the discovery of the telescope would not have known about planetary bodies beyond Saturn.

The hours were assigned planetary rulers as well. Just like the days, the hourly sequence starts with Saturn at the start of the ancient week on Saturday (Saturn's day) and goes on to the moon, then repeats over the twenty-four-hour period.

Gathering plants according to the planetary hours is based on a system thought to have originated with the Babylonian system of astrology and carried over to Greece. Planning your harvesting around planetary correspondences is certainly easier to do than trying to track when the moon will be in the right zodiac sign and planetary ruler. Need some juniper? Go out on a Sunday to cut some. Ideally, you would also want to plan your harvest to happen in the first or eighth hour of that day.

That bit about the hours is somewhat complicated. The Sun rules Sunday with twelve "hours" of daylight and twelve "hours" of dark. The complicated bit is that the "hours" aren't always sixty minutes long except around the spring and fall equinoxes. As the days get longer and the nights get shorter (or vice versa), you have to take the total minutes of daylight or nighttime and divide by twelve. That means on the summer solstice, for example, the day is fourteen to fifteen hours long depending on where you live in the continential United States. This will vary in other areas around the globe as well.

In my area, the summer solstice day is roughly fourteen hours long. That is 840 minutes divided by 12, giving us 70 minutes in each "hour" of daylight. To calculate when the sun is its first hour on a Sunday (assuming Sunday falls around the summer solstice), you start at sunrise at 6:09 a.m. Seventy minutes later (7:19 a.m.) you will be in the second hour of the day, which is ruled by Venus.

To get to the eighth hour of the day, you multiply 70 by eight and come up with 560 minutes, roughly 9.3 standard hours later in the day. That would put the eighth hour at roughly at 3:20 p.m. If this sounds complicate, it is. Fortunately there are plenty of books and apps out there that will do the calculations for you. For convenience, I've included daytime and nighttime charts here for quick reference.

Daytime Hours Chart

Hour	Sunday	Monday	Tuesday	Wednesday	Thursday	Friday	Saturday
1	Sun	Moon	Mars	Mercury	Jupiter	Venus	Saturn
2	Venus	Saturn	Sun	Moon	Mars	Mercury	Jupiter
3	Mercury	Jupiter	Venus	Saturn	Sun	Moon	Mars
4	Moon	Mars	Mercury	Jupiter	Venus	Saturn	Sun
5	Saturn	Sun	Moon	Mars	Mercury	Jupiter	Venus
6	Jupiter	Venus	Saturn	Sun	Moon	Mars	Mercury
7	Mars	Mercury	Jupiter	Venus	Saturn	Sun	Moon
8	Sun	Moon	Mars	Mercury	Jupiter	Venus	Saturn
9	Venus	Saturn	Sun	Moon	Mars	Mercury	Jupiter
10	Mercury	Jupiter	Venus	Saturn	Sun	Moon	Mars
11	Moon	Mars	Mercury	Jupiter	Venus	Saturn	Sun
12	Saturn	Sun	Moon	Mars	Mercury	Jupiter	Venus

Nighttime Hours Chart

Hour	Sunday	Monday	Tuesday	Wednesday	Thursday	Friday	Saturday
1	Jupiter	Venus	Saturn	Sun	Moon	Mars	Mercury
2	Mars	Mercury	Jupiter	Venus	Saturn	Sun	Moon
3	Sun	Moon	Mars	Mercury	Jupiter	Venus	Saturn
4	Venus	Saturn	Sun	Moon	Mars	Mercury	Jupiter
5	Mercury	Jupiter	Venus	Saturn	Sun	Moon	Mars
6	Moon	Mars	Mercury	Jupiter	Venus	Saturn	Sun
7	Saturn	Sun	Moon	Mars	Mercury	Jupiter	Venus
8	Jupiter	Venus	Saturn	Sun	Moon	Mars	Mercury
9	Mars	Mercury	Jupiter	Venus	Saturn	Sun	Moon
10	Sun	Moon	Mars	Mercury	Jupiter	Venus	Saturn
11	Venus	Saturn	Sun	Moon	Mars	Mercury	Jupiter
12	Mercury	Jupiter	Venus	Saturn	Sun	Moon	Mars

As a quick reference, here is a list of the plants covered in this book by planetary influences:

Sun: Juniper, oak, sweet gum, walnut, chicory

Mercury: Clover, fern

Venus: Mugwort, cherry, daisy, fleabane, geranium, periwinkle, violet, plantain

Mars: Holly, onion, poke, thistle, pine

Jupiter: Honeysuckle, dandelion

Saturn: Boxwood, mullein, ivy, mimosa, morning glory

Moon: Chickweed, club moss, moss, willow

Grass presents a bit of a challenge. Different grasses are assigned to different planetary rulers. For example, lemongrass (*Cymbopogon citratus*) is assigned to Mercury. Witchgrass, which is also called dog grass or couch grass (*Agropyron repens*), is assigned to Jupiter. Mondo grass (*Ophiopogon japonicus*) is ascribed to Mars. If your spell calls for grass, you will have to do a little personal research to figure out which one is required. That will tell you which planetary influence is indicated.

Which Is Better?

Let me step back to the original question. Which system for collecting plants is better? In her book *Making Magick*, Edain McCoy states emphatically that working by the moon is most appropriate for magick.[15] The moon governs magick—particularly what is refered to as "low magick"—that is, magick done for

---

15. Edain McCoy, *Making Magick: What It Is and How It Works* (St. Paul, MN: Llewellyn Publications, 1997), 101.

practical purposes using natural materials. Honestly, this book is geared toward those interested in practicing low magick.

The alternative, high magick, is more heavily involved with astrology and planetary movements. High magick is more structured as with alchemy and hermetic traditions. It is generally thought to have as its purpose the goal of enhancing spiritual growth and development. It's not that high magick practitioners didn't use herbs and resins in their workings—they did—but the intent was different, focused on rarifying the soul to bring it in tune with higher celestial forces or contacting otherworldly spirits. Witches may say, "As above, so below," when doing their incantations, but it has an entirely different purpose when uttered by an alchemist.

Life should be in balance. If it is possible to schedule your harvests to accommodate both lunar and solar concerns, that is awesome. I'm afraid in our hectic modern world, most of us will default to planetary correspondences because it is easier make time on a Tuesday to gather ferns than to wait for the moon to transit into Gemini or Virgo during a waxing cycle.

Coordinating Herbs and Elemental Influences

Before you move on to collect your herbs, let's consider how to blend them. There are no hard and fast rules here, at least as far as I am aware. I would not mix scrying herbs (generally governed by Saturn) with herbs for conflict (generally governed by Mars), but you may have a different experience.

I haven't talked about elemental influences yet. According to Agrippa, "He which shall know these qualities of the elements, and their mixations, shall easily bring to pass such things that are wonderful and astonishing, and shall be perfect in magick."[16] The elements have some mixture of hot, dry, cold, and wet.

Fire: Hot, dry

Earth: Cold, dry

Air: Hot, wet

Water: Cold, wet

Generally speaking, herbs with planetary rulers with the same element will work well together. The planets have the following elemental correspondences:

Fire: Mars, Sun (sometimes Jupiter)

Earth: Saturn, Venus

Air: Jupiter, Mercury

Water: Moon (sometimes Saturn)

With this in mind, using our list of herbs, you can see combining cherry, violet, and mugwort for a scrying incense for romantic issues would be good. All these herbs are governed by Venus, which is associated with earth.

Fire and air herbs complement each other, as do water and earth herbs. In other words, they work well together. For example, fern (Mercury, air) and juniper (Sun, fire) would work well together. Ivy (Saturn, earth) and moss (moon, water) would work well together.

---

16. Agrippa, *Three Books of Occult Philosophy*, 8.

Fire and water cancel each other out. For example, chickweed (moon) and chicory (sun) would tend to counteract each other. One is for love and lunar magick. The other is for cursing and removing obstacles. It's hard to see a reason to combine them. Maybe to curse someone with love? It makes no sense.

Earth and air are so opposite it's hard to see how you would bring them together either. Earth is cold and dry; air is hot and wet. Trying to get them to work together is counterintuitive.

To carry this a step futher, fire is opposed by water, complemented by air, and indifferent to earth. Earth is opposed by air, complemented by water, and indifferent to fire. Air is opposed by earth, complemented by fire, and indifferent to water. Finally, water is opposed by fire, complemented by earth, and indifferent to air.

Element	Opposed By	Complemented By	Indifferent To
Fire	Water	Air	Earth
Earth	Air	Water	Fire
Air	Earth	Fire	Water
Water	Fire	Earth	Air

You can combine herbs from all four catagories because this creates a balance. Otherwise, try to use herbs together that complement, not conflict with, each other.

I've compiled a little cheat sheet for the herbs discussed in this book that breaks down the plants by elements:

> *Fire:* Holly, juniper, oak, onion, poke, sweet gum, thistle, walnut
>
> *Earth:* Boxwood, grass, honeysuckle, mugwort, plantain

Air: Chicory, clover, dandelion, fern, mullein, pine

Water: Cherry, chickweed, club moss, daisy, fleabane, geranium, ivy, mimosa, morning glory, moss, periwinkle, violet, willow

CHAPTER 4

From Harvest Prep to Harvesting

You've considered your purpose. You've determined what plants will suit that purpose. You've consulted the charts and picked the right time to gather the material. It's time to gear up. You wouldn't take a camping trip without packing the tent, lanterns, sleeping bags, and food. You wouldn't head off to an important presentation at work without your notes and your flowcharts.

You can keep an eye open for plants to use on a casual walk around the yard or a bike trip along a country field you have legal access to. You don't need much gear for that—maybe a notepad or a phone camera. When you are ready to harvest, you'll need a few things and a few last considerations before going out to collect.

Tools

Blades

Something to cut with is a good place to start. Traditionally, an athame or boline is used. An athame is a ceremonial knife. Some Pagans sharpen their athames. Others prefer to leave the edge dull to support the notion of symbolism. Athames, in some traditions, aren't meant to be used for cutting in the mundane world. They are "knives" in the spiritual or ceremonial world only. You will be gathering herbs for ritual purposes, but does that qualify as a reason to take your athame from your altar out into the mundane world? You are the only one who can make that call.

Fortunately, there is a cutting tool available to us. It is the boline. The boline can be a straight-edge knife with a white handle, or it can be a sickle-shaped blade, the handle of which can be made of varying materials. Mine happens to be made of brass with a bloodstone inset in the handle. Most traditions seem to accept that using the boline in the real world is not only okay, but that's what it was designed for.

Some practices prescribe a silver or gold knife to collect herbs. Pliny the Elder wrote about Druids gathering mistletoe with a golden knife or sickle in the first century CE in his book *Natural History*.[17] If you are so fortunate as to be able to afford a golden knife, bless your heart! Go for it.

Pruners

From my perspective as a long-time gardener, there's nothing wrong with using a common pair of pruners that you can get at any garden or hardware store. Once gathered, the herbs will be consecrated later. I personally believe no desecration occurs when I use gardening tools for gathering my magickal herbs.

Pruners typically are either scissor blades or bypass or anvil-cut pruners. Scissor blades are just what they sound like—they have two sharp blades that cut by passing each other just like the scissors you use in the kitchen or at the office. A bypass pruner

---

17. Pliny the Elder, *Natural History*, trans. John Bostock and H. T. Riley (London: Henry G. Bohn, 1855), bk. 16, ch. 95.

has one sharp blade that moves in a scissor-like action past a curved bar.

Anvil-cut pruners have a single sharp blade that cuts through the material and comes to rest on a flat bar. Think of this cutting action as being similar to using a kitchen knife and a cutting board. Scissor blades will give a cleaner cut, but the size of stem they will sever is limited.

Bypass and anvil pruners may bruise the stem of the plant you are working on, especially if you are trying to cut a large stem. This is a consideration if you are pruning a rose bush or other landscape plant. However, it should not be a problem when gathering herbs because you will be dicing up the plant material anyway.

Digging Tools

You will need something to dig for roots. If you are working in your yard or close to home, any type of shovel will do. When going on field trips into the woods or roadside, short-handled trowels are much easier to carry along than a long-handled shovel.

Plant Containers

Next, you need some sort of bag to put your harvest in. These can be old grocery bags or plastic storage bags—whatever works for you. You won't be keeping your herbs in these once they've been processed. You'll also need something to carry all this in. I like a backpack, but you can use whatever you're comfortable with.

Writing Tools

You will need paper and something with which to write. For practical purposes, it helps to make a note of what you've gathered. If you are harvesting several different types of roots, they can begin to look a lot alike. Keep your plants separate and label each bag.

You may want to carry a notebook or journal to record where you found your plants for future reference. You may see a plant that isn't quite ready, and you want to remember where it is located for a future harvest. Or you may simply be inspired to write a little poetry or make note of something that motivated you while you were out on your walk. Walks with nature have a habit of doing that to us.

Camera

If you have a digital camera or camera phone, this is a great opportunity to gather pictures of your world too. It's another handy way to document what stage a plant is in or where you might have found it.

Clothing

What about clothing? Pliny the Elder wrote that ancient Druids went out in white robes to gather mistletoe with great ceremony.[18] In *The Book of the Sacred Magic of Abramelin the Mage*, every magickal activity is done in special clothing that is kept clean and used for no other purpose.[19]

I don't know of any modern witches who go to these extents. I will talk in a few pages about the act of cutting a plant, which does involve special considerations. Dress is not a special consideration. If you are gathering plants around the home, wear comfortable clothing and shoes. If you are gathering plants from

18. Pliny the Elder, *Natural History*, bk. 16, ch. 95.
19. *The Book of the Sacred Magic of Abramelin the Mage*, trans. by S. L. MacGregor Mathers (New York: Dover Publications, 1975), 68.

nearby woods, definitely wear solid shoes. I occasionally take people on field trips to point out usable magickal plants. I always advise the attendees to wear sturdy shoes. Someone always shows up in flip-flops or dress slippers. All I can say to them is, "Bless your little heart. Try to keep up."

Do I need to tell anyone in the day of Lyme disease or encephalitis-carrying mosquitoes to take along some form of bug repellant? Bugs abound and they've got to eat too. Unfortunately, what some of them eat is us.

Health experts at the Centers for Disease Control say that when you venture outside, you should ideally wear long-sleeved shirts and long pants with the ends tucked into your socks or boots.[20] A show of hands, please, of anyone who is likely to do that in the Deep South in the middle of July. Yeah, I thought so. It ain't gonna happen. The experts will also tell us to avoid being out when bugs are active in the early morning hours or early evening hours—in other words, in the coolest part of the day. That means you should all be out gathering herbs at midday—exactly when health experts tell us not to be in the sun due to the skin cancer risk.[21]

Hopefully, you will be able to schedule your plant collections around the appropriate days or hours for the things you hope to harvest. I am well aware that will be hard to do in a modern world. Most of us are going to be out during the day as our schedules permit, whether that is early in the morning or in the middle of the day.

---

20. "Gardening Health and Safety," Centers for Disease Control and Prevention, last modified December 23, 2015, https://www.cdc.gov/family/gardening/index.htm.

21. "Sun Safety," American Skin Association, accessed June 10, 2020, http://www.americanskin.org/resource/safety.php.

Bug Repellent

Wear bug repellant. If you don't believe in DEET-based products, try Buzz Away or Bugz Off. DEET has been around since World War II, when it was developed for the military to be used in jungle conditions. It has been repeatedly tested by both government and medical authorities and approved as safe for use as directed by the manufacturer. Still, I'm aware many of my friends are very averse to using what is basically an insecticide on themselves and their children.

Homemade Insect Repellent

You can also make your own repellent with a blend of lavender, citronella, and eucalyptus essential oils (½ teaspoon each) to four ounces of witch hazel. Keep in mind that most products based on essential oils will not last as long as DEET and will have to be applied every couple of hours.

And don't forget the sunscreen.

Ideal Plant Conditions

Finally, you are ready to gather plants. Specifically, you want the best bits of the plant you intend to harvest, whether it is flower, leaf, or root. You will be using these herbs to honor deities. Do you really think a deity (of any tradition) will be honored to receive bug-riddled leaf or moldy flower? You will be using these herbs to help supply the energy to bring prosperity or a loving companion or to help heal a sick friend. How much energy do you suppose a rotten root has? Not much.

The herbs used, whether while honoring a deity or working a spell, are like tiny batteries. You want them to be fully charged while in their natural state. You will be adding your own energies to them later. For the greatest effect, the plant material must be in good to excellent condition before you harvest it.

Consider the requirements of any of the ancient religions when they performed animal sacrifices. Set aside, for the moment, how you might personally feel about animal sacrifices. The beasts brought to the temple were the best the supplicant had to offer. He or she was making a personal or a family sacrifice in the hopes of receiving the blessing of his or her deity. The idea of bringing a sick animal for sacrifice because doing so would not measurably impact the family's current economic status would have been sacrilege.

Look for the same quality when you gather the herbs you will process for your magickal inventory. Gather the best you can or don't even bother.

Talking to the Plant

The next step can get a bit uncomfortable. The first thing you must do is communicate with the plant. I don't care if you are picking flowers from it, gathering leaves, or digging it up entirely. Communicate your intention, especially if you are harvesting roots. You can gather flowers without harming the plant. You can take leaves without much consequence as long as you don't take too many.

But if you are harvesting roots of small plants, you are killing that plant. A shrub or tree may not be markedly harmed. Taking the roots of something like a mayapple or chicory plant means that plant is not going to survive. The least you can do is tell it why it is dying for you.

Let's go back to our discussion of animal sacrifice. Despite what you typically see in many horror and fantasy films, the animal wasn't dragged to the altar kicking and screaming. It was handled with care and gentleness to keep it as calm as possible. Only then would the energy transfer smoothly, beneficially for the ritual.

Plants don't have the same sentience as people, in my opinion. However, they are not "things" either. When people ask whether any nonhuman thing is self-aware, science tells us, they are anthropomorphizing the nonhuman thing—attributing human emotions and motives to something that clearly isn't human. People do it to everything from cars to stuffed animals.

Pagans tend to believe in plant awareness. Even some scientists have voiced support for the idea. Gustav Theodor Fechner, a German psychologist and father of experimental psychology, believed in panpsychism.[22] He developed his theories between 1860 and the time of his death in 1887. Everything has some degree of mental awareness and spirit, he said, even rocks and plants. Charles Darwin believed too, at least in a limited sort of plant awareness.

The latest researcher to catch the public's imagination in regard to the ability of plants, specifically trees, to create communities and to "care" about others in that community is Peter Wohlleben. In 2016, he published *The Hidden Life of Trees*, based on his work as a forestry researcher.[23] In it, he proposed that trees

22. Frederick C. Beiser, "Gustav Theodor Fechner," *The Stanford Encyclopedia of Philosophy*, January 12, 2020, https://plato.stanford.edu/archives /spr2020/entries/fechner/. English translations of Fechner's book, *Nanna oder über das Seelenleben der Pflanzen* (Nanna, or the soul-life of plants; Leipzig, 1848), are hard to find. However, an online translation is available as of June 11, 2020, at https://en.calameo.com/books /00453793521ca73748e66.

23. Peter Wohlleben, *The Hidden Life of Trees: What They Feel, How They Communicate—Discoveries from a Secret World* (Vancouver, Canada: Graystone Books, 2016).

form communities, nurture each other, and even warn others in danger of attack. The book caused quite a stir by expressing an opinion that many Pagans would heartily agree with.

I have never met an Ent or Huorn in my walks through the landscape or the woods. I have felt the energy of the plant kingdom wherever I have encountered plants. I think plants can experience distress. I don't think plants feel in the same way people do. At least, I hope they don't. What a terrible world that would be! Imagine the horror of being tied to one spot and experiencing the menacing blade of a lawn mower week after week as it cruelly slices away one-third of your existence with every whorl of the blade. Imagine the sorrow of knowing that thousands and thousands of your offspring will fall to your roots, never reaching their full potential. Or the ravages of bugs and squirrels and fungi that relentlessly gnaw at your body.

Regardless, plants are a living part of this thing Pagans call the World Web. They play a part from which everyone can benefit mightily. For that reason, I strongly recommend you communicate with the plant you intend to harvest.

The Greek Magickal Papyri are a good place to start if you have never considered talking to the plant you mean to harvest from. In the section labeled PGM IV. 286–95, the mage is instructed to say:

> I am picking you, such and such a plant (say the name of the plant), with my five-fingered hand, I, NN (your name), and I am bringing you home so that you may work for me for a certain purpose. I adjure you by the undefiled / name of the god: if you pay no heed to me, the earth which produced you will no longer be watered as far as you are concerned—

ever in life again, if I fail in this operation, MOLITHABAR NACH BARNACHÕCHA BRAEÕ MENDA LAUBRAASSE PHASPHA BENDÕ; fulfil for me the perfect charm.[24]

The words in capital letters are thought to be the names of demons, angel, and or deities that would have been familiar to practitioners in ancient Egypt. Here is another example from the same book in PGM IV. 2967–3006:

The invocation for him, which he speaks over any herb, generally at the moment of picking, is as follows:

"You were sown by Kronos, you were conceived by Hera, / you were maintained by Ammon, you were given birth by Isis, you were nourished by Zeus the god of rain, you were given growth by Helios and dew. You [are] the dew of all the gods, you are the heart of Hermes, you are the seed of the primordial gods, you are the eye / of Helios, you are the light of Selene, you are the zeal of Osiris, you are the beauty and glory of Ouranos, you are the soul of Osiris' daimon which revels in every place, you are the spirit of Ammon. As you have exalted Osiris, so / exalt yourself and rise just as Helios rises each day. Your size is equal to the zenith of Helios, your roots come from the depths, but your powers are in the heart of Hermes, your fibers are the bones of Mnevis, and your / flowers are the eye of Horus, your seed is Pan's seed. I am washing you in resin as I also wash the gods even [as I do this] for my own health. You also be cleaned by prayer and give us power as Ares and Athena do. I am Hermes. I am acquir-

---

24. Hans Dieter Betz, ed., *The Greek Magical Papyri in Translation*, 2nd ed. (Chicago: University of Chicago Press, 1992), 43–44 (parentheses mine).

ing you with Good / Fortune and Good Daimon both at a propitious hour and on a propitious day that is effective for all things."[25]

When the mage is finished, he gathers up the harvested material and leaves an offering of wheat and barley seeds mixed with honey.[26]

Notice what is going on here. The magician begins by praising the plant, making comparisons to all the deities he knows. That may sound like certain Pagan rituals when Pagans speak adorations to the deities and spirits who have been invited to the ritual or circle. Here the magician also is expressing his understanding of the parts of the plant that are governed by each of the deities, demonstrating his knowledge and expertise.

These spells are thought to have been written and collected sometime between 100 BCE and 400 CE. He is explaining what he plans to do with the material. Before he leaves, he makes an offering in place of the material he has taken. Does this sound familiar? Is this not exactly what I am writing about today?

Personally, I like that I am doing something that people have been doing for centuries—communicating with and respectfully utilizing plants. Still, I understand. Some people aren't sure how to talk to plants. Others think it downright silly. I've done it for so many years it's second nature.

You can communicate with the plant in whatever manner feels right to you. What you say can be as elaborate or as simple as you like. It can be spoken out loud or in silent prayer. It helps to ask for the plant's help and tell it what you intend to use it for.

25. Dieter Betz, ed., *The Greek Magical Papyri in Translation*, 95 (brackets Dieter Betz's).

26. Dieter Betz, ed., *The Greek Magical Papyri in Translation*, 95.

Author Scott Cunningham gives us guidance on how to speak to plants while gathering. He was a popular occult writer in the 1990s who wrote a series of books that helped make Wicca more accessible to the general public, especially for solitary practitioners. In one of his books, he tells us one old grimoire recommends saying to periwinkle as it is gathered, "I pray thee, vinca pervinca, thee that art to be had for thy many useful qualities, that thou come to me glad blossoming with thy mainfulness."[27] If that's the way you talk, go on ahead.

I tend to approach a plant like this: "Hey, baby. I need your help. Just a little bit of your leaves for this spell to help me focus my energies for a special project." And then I thank the plant. Sometimes I speak out loud. Sometimes I simply think my intention. It all depends on the mood.

Gathering the Plant

If you are gathering flowers, pinch the blossom off just below the base of the blossom. This is a technique called "dead-heading" in the gardening community. Dead-heading means removing a faded flower. Of course, the blossom you are picking is probably not going to be faded. Flowers for magick are best picked at the height of their glory, but the technique is the same.

To gather a few leaves, pinch or cut them off right at the point where the leaf joins the branch. To take a branch, you will definitely need a pair of pruners. Most wands are made of wood that is about the diameter of your forefinger—a bit too big to cut with a boline or athame.

---

27. Scott Cunningham, *Cunningham's Encyclopedia of Magical Herbs* (St. Paul, MN: Llewellyn Publications, 2002), 201.

Prune a branch at a lateral—the point where it forks away from another branch or the main trunk of the tree. Make a quick, clean cut at a 45-degree angle. A slanted cut means water won't stay on the cut, increasing the chance of decay. It means the cut should dry and scale over. Don't worry about painting something over the cut. Trees and shrubs have defense mechanisms to take care of themselves if you do this right.

When you are done, give thanks and offer something in return. I sometimes take time to help scatter the plant's seeds if the time of year is right. Another way of offering tribute is to leave something sustaining behind. I sometimes bring a little honey with me. That feeds the local wildlife and insect population that helps nurture the local environment. Some folks like to leave birdseed. Just be aware that seeds can sprout, and you may be introducing something alien into the local environment. A better choice might be processed nuts. These won't sprout but will feed the locals.

There is something else that I would like to stress. Never take more than you need. Never take more than a third of a plant or a third of a colony (if your need is great) in any case. Being a responsible land steward means that you have to allow plants the opportunity to survive. If you want to be practical, this approach means you will have a source for future harvests. If you want to be ethical, this approach illustrates that you have no right to wipe out a species for your own selfish needs, even if we are talking about doing so just in your immediate area.

CHAPTER 5
Processing Your Plants

Now that you have your herbs, it's time to process them. As you gathered your herbs, you had in mind your purpose. You communicated this to the plant and thanked it. As you process the herbs, that purpose really should be in mind. If you are just mechanically going through the motions, you might as well be cooking dinner.

I don't advocate making flowery speeches while you work any more than I recommend flowery speeches while collecting herbs. You don't have to be in a religious fervor. But never let your purpose stray too far from your mind as you work.

The question arises, should you chop first and then dry or dry first and then chop? This can be a bit tricky. Roots should definitely be cut into smaller pieces before drying. You can dry a whole root, but it takes longer, and the end result is going to be very, very hard to cut up. These things have a tendency to get as hard as a brickbat once they're dried.

Small leaves and flowers don't have to be broken up. They can go straight to the drying process. I like to dry large leaves first, then break them up. It is simply easier. You won't be drying your herbs to a crisp, but they will be more pliable after drying. I suggest you experiment and see what works best for you.

If I were talking about culinary herbs, I would recommend drying, then chopping. Preserving the essential oils is critical when processing cooking herbs. If you chop first, you are opening up more areas through which those oils can be lost. This is not an important issue for our magickal herbs. Remember, I said that herbs you may have gathered beyond your control may have harmful chemicals on them or in them. You should not be consuming them in any form.

If you have gathered the herbs from your own property or from an area where you are positive about what has or has not been applied to the plant, you have the discretion to make the choice yourself.

Chopping

Start by cutting the material up into little pieces. How little should the pieces be? I recommend taking them down to the size of your little fingernail. This will be a workable size for use in gris-gris bags, witch bottles, or small herb packets that you intend to burn or bury.

Should you need to make the pieces smaller for use as an incense or in a really small charm, you can always process the herbs further at the time you are making those items.

You may find, especially with large leaves, that the leaf veins are hard and unyielding. Even after drying, these parts will be hard to process down to a powder. For example, some thistle leaves have heavy veins or ribs. In this case, use a pair of scissors to cut the rib out before chopping. The rib can be discarded in the compost pile or taken back to nature to decompose.

Drying

A slow, steady drying process is best. If you have a warm attic, that is ideal. The best drying setup I ever had was in the boiler room at a senior adult facility where I worked as a gardener. Winter or summer, if I spread any flowers or leaves out to dry on an old window screen for a future craft project, the material was thoroughly desiccated within two days.

If you don't have an attic or a boiler room, there are other options. We all know how hot it can be inside a car, especially in summer. Try putting your herbs in the car's back window ledge. Make certain you layer the material between paper towels or newspapers so that the herbs don't stain the car fabric. Leaves and flowers can dry in as little as one afternoon. Roots may take a little bit longer. Just don't drive off with the windows down or all your efforts may be lost.

A little less exotic drying tool is the oven or microwave. A gas-powered oven is ideal because it often takes no more than the pilot light to slowly dry your herbs to perfection. Leave the door open a crack to help the process. An electric oven works too. Set it on the lowest possible setting. Check your herbs frequently, especially if you are new to this. You don't want to bake the herbs to a cinder. You will also need to stir or turn the plant material from time to time to ensure even drying.

In a pinch, you can use a microwave. Lay the leaves or flowers between a couple of paper towels. Put in the oven and microwave for about thirty seconds to one minute. Microwaves vary in strength, so you will have to experiment. Take the herbs out and test for dryness. The material should be just brittle. Repeat, if necessary, for another thirty seconds or so.

Of course, you can use a food dryer too. This appliance is very good because it provides slow, steady heat without tying up your oven. Because most dehydrators come with grate-like trays, you will probably want to dry your herbs first and then chop them up.

I find that the color and texture of the herbs, particularly flowers, is better when I use a dehydrator, but use whatever method you have available. The end result is the same. Your herbs should now be ready to use immediately or to store for later use.

Be aware that it takes a little practice to know when your herbs are fully dried. You may think you have the job done, put the herbs away in storage containers, and come back at a later time and find a moldy, mildewed mess. If you are doing this for the first time and intend to store your herbs for later, it pays to check them every few days for a couple of weeks to make certain the plant material is truly dry.

Storing

Once dried and properly stored, herbs should last for six to twelve months. As in the kitchen, any herbs held longer than that will have lost most of their potency regardless of how well you process them. Resins are the exception. These seem to hold indefinitely, from my experience. Flowers, leaves, and even roots will tend to become stale after twelve months.

Does this matter? You may wonder, "If I charge the herbs periodically, won't they still be potent?"

I'll talk in a moment about charging plant material. You can charge herbs like clockwork; it won't stop time, and it won't keep the herbs from becoming stale eventually. Everything goes back to the universe in its own time. I have said frequently that to honor a deity appropriately or to perform strong magick, you need the best material possible. Stale herbs don't fall into this category. Inventory your herbs on a regular basis. Toss what is bad and collect more if you need it.

I hold herbs in a variety of ways. A practical way to store your herbs is in plastic bags. Vacuum plastic food storage bags work very well. Ziplock bags are okay, but keep in mind they don't always do a good job of keeping air and moisture out.

I like to use attractive screw-top jars and display my herbs on a shelf. This gives you an opportunity to be creative by decorating your containers. Just keep your herbs out of direct sunlight. Direct sunlight will hasten the breakdown of your herbs.

I have known witches who are sticklers for precision and organization. When they need jars for their herbs, they go to a store (or the internet) and order a particular size and style of glass container. They carefully paint the herb names on the jar or print attractive labels. Their herb collection is a beauty to behold and a great source of pride. As well it should be.

You don't have to go to that type of expense. Some food and beverage manufacturers get very creative with the containers they put their products in. I have a couple of friends who make and sell a variety of magickal oils. They use the most delightful wine and liquor bottles to hold and age their oils. The bottles are covered in magickal symbols to help reinforce their intent.

I like to haunt thrift shops and flea markets for interesting containers. These can be bottles that formerly held exotic oils or candies or cookies. Sometimes the bottles are molded into a shape that is perfect for a particular herb. For example, the myrrh resin in my herb cabinet is stored in a red, heart-shaped container that probably held cinnamon heart candy at some point. Myrrh is a sweet herb of peace and spirituality. It is right where it should be in a heart-shaped container.

Like my friends, you can reinforce the energy of your herbs by painting appropriate symbols on the containers. This will also help shield them from sunlight if the container happens to be clear. The symbols could be Nordic runes or Celtic Oghams. They can be the sign of the planetary ruler or the elements. You can use the signs and symbols used in modern-day life, such as hearts, peace signs, smiley faces, lightning bolts, and symbols for moon phases. You can simply paint the container with an appropriate color, such as red for passion and gold for prosperity. If you're really ambitious and talented, paint totem figures on the container, such as dragons for fiery energy and gnomes for earth energy.

Or you can simply label the containers. Nothing says you have to put anything other than a name on the container. But please do put a name on the container. You may think you will be able to distinguish dried nightshade from dried mugwort. Trust me. You probably won't.

Consecrating

One final step is helpful before you put your herbs away. Take time to consecrate your herbs. You can do this just prior to using the plant material too. However, it doesn't hurt to take some time for this effort when you have first finished processing the material.

Work with herbs that have similar properties if you have a variety. Don't try to energize herbs for love in the same ritual in which you energize herbs for banishing. Energizing can be done generally during a waxing moon for herbs with positive energies or during a waning moon for herbs with negative energies. Remember, positive and negative don't mean good and evil. For me, the terms indicate the difference between open, welcoming, inviting activities and secretive, protective, controlling activities.

To be really specific, you can energize your herbs on the night and in the hour of the planet that governs them. This requires very careful planning and a real dedication of time and effort. The premise is that such dedication will come through in your magick.

Take a moment to consider what energy you want to raise. Is it love? Do you need a peaceful energy for meditations? Is it a growing energy for increase or a protective energy to shield? Linger on that intention. What color is it? How do you feel when you experience it? If it has an associated smell, what would it be? Can you imagine how love or increase or protection or peace tastes? Bring as many senses as you can imagine into play.

Set up your altar according to your custom. Don't forget to bring your prepared herbs. Use color-specific candles. Black (for negative) or white (for positive) candles can be used in lieu of color-specific candles. Cast a circle in the time and place of your choosing. Light appropriate incense. Evoke your guardians. Light your candles and call your patron deities for assistance. You can also call upon deities specific to the energy you need in place of patron deities.

Now move. Walk around your circle deosil if you are working on positive energies or widdershins if the energy needed should be negative. Dance if that is your habit. When limited space prohibits walking or dancing, sway or rock. Focus on your intent. Sing or hum or silently repeat your intent, even it is just saying "protect" or "love" or "growth" over and over again. Hold your container(s) of herbs as you chant or let your hands hover over the herbs. Gently stroke the herbs for love, spirituality, and compassion. Hold the herbs for protection firmly; don't be afraid to shake or rattle them.

Let the energy build until you feel motivated to send that energy into your herbs. Be confident that you will know when that point in time is. You may find it helpful to create a loud sound when you are ready to send out the energy. This can be done by ringing a bell or hitting a gong or loudly clapping your hands or shouting, "It is done!" or "Huzzah!" or whatever the spirit moves you to shout.

Once you've completed the task, pause. Ground yourself. Sense the ambience of your circle. Know that you have worked magick—created a living battery, as it were, with the herbs you have empowered. They will be available for you to tap in the future.

Thank the deities you invited to the circle and ask them for permission to call upon them in the future. Do the same with your guardians. Open the circle.

Now you're ready to use the herbs that you have personally gathered. In the next section on plants, you have roughly thirty-two new spells and crafts to add to those you may already have in your repertoire. With just the few dozen plants described here, you can create magickal tools like besoms and inks, conjure healing energies, enhance your personal prosperity, and more.

PART TWO

THE PLANTS

CHAPTER 6

Learning about Common Plants

Now I am ready to talk about some of the plants you can find in your immediate area.

Some of these plants are native to America. Others were introduced. Some are cousins of plants that would have been familiar to people from Europe, Africa, or Asia before they immigrated to the New World. A few would have been brand new to our old-world ancestors but were close enough in form or effect to something they knew that the new plant adopted the associations of the old-world plants.

To keep track of them all, you need a very basic understanding of the way plants are categorized or named. I have shelves of gardening books, most of which touch to some degree on the topic of plant names. However, I am predominately referencing Peter McHoy's *Anatomy of a Garden* for this brief discussion.[28]

After being classified as vascular (with special tissues to transport water, etc.) and nonvascular (without said system), plants are divided into either angiosperm (flowering) plants, such as clover or cherries, or gymnosperm (nonflowering) like

28. Peter McHoy, *Anatomy of a Garden* (New York: Gallery Books, 1987), 60.

pines. The majority of plants fall into the flowering category with some further division into monocot (one seed leaf on sprouting) or dicot (two seed leaves on sprouting). Most grasses are moncots; almost everything else is dicot.

Plants fall into 620 families, at last count. I will be mainly concerned with just a few of those families like the rose family (Rosaceae) and the aster family (Asteraceae). After the family name, plants that share common characteristics are assigned a genus and a species name. The species name is often descriptive. Take for example *Artemisia vulgaris*, or mugwort. *Artemisia* is the genus and *vulgaris* is a Latin word for "coarse," referring to the texture of the plant. In another example, *Viola odorata*, the Latin name for a type of violet gives us the genus, *Viola*, followed by the descriptor, *odorata*, meaning "sweet smelling."

This is the binomial Linnaean system I mentioned earlier, named after Carl von Linné, who came up with the system. Beyond that, plants may have a varietal name. These are usually cultivated plants or plants that someone has brought into existence by purposefully crossing one plant with another.

For example, in the Rosaceae family, there are five well-known genera (*Prunus, Malus, Crataegus, Sorbus,* and *Rosa*). The genus *Rosa* has eleven subtypes and more species and subspecies than you can shake a stick at. But among those are modern garden roses, and in that category, you can find the cultivar group hybrid tea rose, and in that group you will find lovely flowers like the 'Peace' rose, or *Rosa* 'Peace'.

When you see an × in a botanical name, that means two species within the same family have been crossbred.

Researchers are often recategorizing plants as methods and tools improve. When that happens, sometimes plants get moved from one classification to another. For example, in my 2002 edition of *Cunningham's Encyclopedia of Magical Herbs*, the common field daisy is listed as *Chrysanthemum leucanthemum*.[29] It is now classified as *Leucanthemum vulgare*, and *Chrysanthemum leucanthemum* is considered a synonym. Cunningham wrote his original text in 1985. Things change.

Late in 2019, the Royal Horticultural Society of England determined that the category *Rosmarinus officialis* is no longer appropriate when talking about "the dew of the sea" (the original translation of *Rosmarinus*).[30] After detailed DNA analysis, researchers have determined that rosemary should join the sage genus of plants. It is now *Salvia rosmarinus*. If you haven't seen the change in literature or plant tags, wait for it. It's coming.

You don't need any of this botanical information to create magickal spells. However, it will be helpful when you gather plants to help you to understand the material you are picking, to compare and contrast plants in the same genus and to ensure you are gathering the correct plant for your work.

I've tried to select thirty-two relatively common plants that should be available across the continental US in most plant hardiness zones. These zones are designated by the US Department of Agriculture to indicate what plants are likely to grow in a particular area based on the plants' cold tolerance. There are eleven zones that will take you from an average winter cold temperature of minus 60 degrees to 60 degrees above 0. I've included a map that is current as of this writing, but you can also find an interactive map at https://planthardiness.ars.usda.gov/PHZMWeb/.

---

29. Cunningham, *Cunningham's Encyclopedia of Magical Herbs*, 98.
30. "Rosemary Becomes a Sage," Royal Horticultural Society, December 2019, https://www.rhs.org.uk/plants/articles/misc/rosemary-becomes-a-sage.

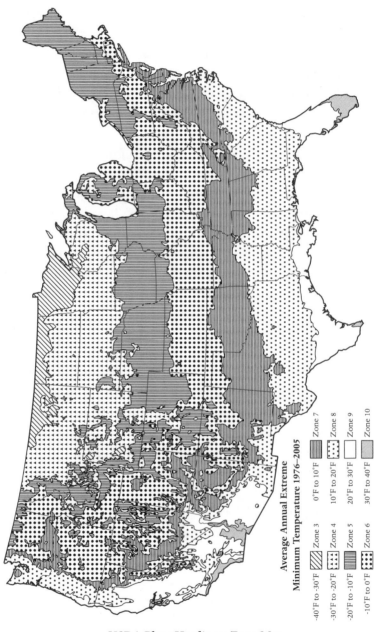

Average Annual Extreme
Minimum Temperature 1976–2005

-40°F to -30°F Zone 3   0°F to 10°F Zone 7

-30°F to -20°F Zone 4   10°F to 20°F Zone 8

-20°F to -10°F Zone 5   20°F to 30°F Zone 9

-10°F to 0°F Zone 6   30°F to 40°F Zone 10

USDA Plant Hardiness Zone Map

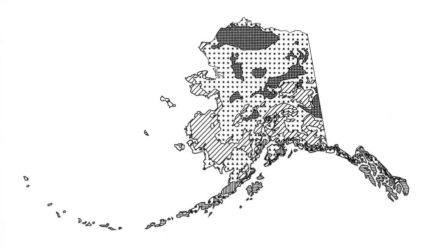

**Average Annual Extreme
Minimum Temperature 1976–2005**

-60°F to -50°F ▓ Zone 1   10°F to 20°F ⦂⦂ Zone 8

-50°F to -40°F ⦂⦂ Zone 2   20°F to 30°F ☐ Zone 9

-40°F to -30°F ▨ Zone 3   30°F to 40°F ▨ Zone 10

-30°F to -20°F ▲▲ Zone 4   40°F to 50°F ▨ Zone 11

-20°F to -10°F ▥ Zone 5   50°F to 60°F ▤ Zone 12

-10°F to 0°F ⦂⦂ Zone 6   60°F to 70°F ▓ Zone 13

0°F to 10°F ▤ Zone 7

USDA Plant Hardiness Zone Map Continued

l information provided for each plant includes the
r, where you are likely to find it, the parts you will
gather, what you can use each plant for, and any special
precaution about toxicity.

I mentioned earlier that most people have a few basic needs
in mind when they do magick. You may find this breakdown of
the plants covered in this book to be a handy cheat sheet for your
purposes:

> *Exorcism:* Clover, fern, juniper, mullein, onion, pine,
> poke, thistle, witchgrass, sweet gum
>
> *Health:* Fern, ivy, mugwort, mullein, oak, onion, pine,
> thistle, walnut
>
> *Love:* Cherry, clover, geranium, juniper, male fern,
> mimosa, onion, periwinkle, violet, witchgrass
>
> *Luck:* Clover, fern, holly, moss, oak, violet
>
> *Prosperity:* Clover, fern, honeysuckle, moss, onion, per-
> iwinkle, pine, oak
>
> *Protection:* Clover, fern, fleabane, geranium, grass, hon-
> eysuckle, mimosa, onion, periwinkle, moss, sweet
> gum, thistle, violet
>
> *Spirit:* Cherry, dandelion, honeysuckle, mimosa, mug-
> wort, thistle

Right away, you may notice that several of these herbs have
multiple uses. Sometimes, it's not always easy to see an association. I am not surprised that some people come to the conclusion
that the "right" herb isn't really important for magickal workings,
that any herb will do if the intent of the witch is there.

This is where a deep understanding of the herb is important.
For example, a four-leaf clover is a well-known good luck herb.

Four-leaf clovers are rare, so finding one was an automatic sign of good fortune. The four leaves made the form of a cross, a symbol that is signifcant to many traditions. You can readily see how someone might associate good luck with good prosperity. But love? Or protection?

It is the red-flowered clover that helps in love spells. Think "lucky in love." As for protection, the three-leaf clover is a sign of triplicity. That can be the Celtic triplicities of Brigid or the invocation of the powers of land, sky, and sea. Frankly, it can be the Christian triplicity of the Father, Son, and Holy Ghost or God, Jesus, and Mary.

Three is universally significant and found in many cultures, regardless of religion. In numerology, three is the first perfection, followed by six as the second perfection and nine as the final perfection. Psychologists tell us it may be related to the realization in early humans that a basic family unit starts with three. One person is a single unit, the universe made manifest, and masculine in the magickal, not the gender, sense. Two is one reflecting on itself, considering its function and purpose, feminine, and mysterious, again in the magickal and not gender sense. When they combine (procreate), three is created—a family unit, something that requires both one and two to exist but that does not diminish either of the participants—truly magickal.

The following information probably won't answer all your questions about these plants, but it should get you started on your way to wildcrafting in your own area.

BOXWOOD

Latin Name: Buxus

Locations: Foundation plantings

Parts Used: Leaves, wood

Hardiness Zones: 5 to 8

Planetary Ruler: Saturn

Uses: To see the unknown, scrying, funeral rituals,
    magickal tools

Edibility: Inedible

Warning: All parts of this plant are mildly toxic and
    should not be ingested.

Boxwood is an evergreen standard in the landscape. Make
sure the plant you think is boxwood is in fact *Buxus* and not *Ilex*
(holly) or *Ligustrum* (privet).

I have not included privet in this list because, honestly, it is one of the few plants commonly found in the United States for which I can find no magickal correspondence. It is said to have a number of uses in Chinese medicine. Occassionally you will hear old folks call privet "the poor man's boxwood." The small-leaf variety, *L. sinense*, can look a bit like a boxwood from a distance if it is kept pruned into a hedge or rounded shape. Once it is allowed to grow freely, privet can defintely be distinguished from boxwood. It has a more open, loose habit. It flowers in summer with a prominent clusters of fragrant, tiny white flowers followed later in the year by blue-black berries.

Appearance

Boxwoods look quite different from privet. You can find two types of boxwood in the landscape—English and American. Japanese (*B. microphylla*) and Korean boxwood (*B. microphylla* var. *koreana*) are not as commonly found but can been seen in formal knot gardens.

To look at them, you might think English boxwoods and American boxwoods are two different plants in the *Buxus* genus. English boxwoods are naturally more compact and tidy, even when they grow to 8 feet in height. Their leaves are glossy, small and rounded. American boxwoods are more loose and billowy. The foliage is evergreen, a bit more oval than round and has more of a dull green look to it.

Actually, both plants are *Buxus sempervirens*. The difference is that English boxwoods are propagated by cuttings. American boxwoods grow from seeds.

History

You will find boxwoods most often around older homes. At one time, having a healthy stand of English boxwood was a bit of a status symbol. These shrubs grow slowly to about 4 to 6 feet tall and tend to be expensive to purchase. I knew some landscapers in the 1990s who made a pretty penny by convincing new home-owners to allow them to dig up the mature boxwoods around their newly purchased existing home and replace them with more trendy shrubs. As soon as the boxwoods were carefully dug up, the landscapers turned around and sold them for a hefty price to people who knew the true value of the plant!

American boxwoods are more vigorous and can grow to nearly 20 feet in height—much to the chagrin of the homeowner who planted them too close to the foundation of the home. I have never heard of anyone digging up and reselling American boxwoods. If those got dug up, they usually made a short trip to the landfill.

Boxwoods fell out of favor due to problems with leaf miners and nematodes. Leaf miners can be monitored and sprayed for. Boxwood nematodes are a death knell. Homeowners generally would not know the pest was present until their prized boxwoods began to decline in vigor and turn a sickly shade of orange. By then, it was too late. Once established in the soil, only expensive soil drenches could eradicate nematodes. The boxwoods would generally have to be destroyed.

Uses

If you have boxwood around your residence, consider your-self lucky. Boxwood is associated with the underworld and the unknown. It helps us find that which is hidden. Use the leaves in scrying incenses and to guard against negativity. Some of the old grimoires required the mage to use wood from the boxwood plant to make the handle of the athame.

You may have heard the word *psychopomp* or read it in some books on magick. A psychopomp is a deity who moves between the worlds. He or she can descend to the underworld and return to the mundane world or to the heavens, unchallenged. Sometimes the psychopomp is guiding the newly deceased to the underworld. Other times he or she might be carrying messages between worlds. Examples of psychopomps are Hecate, Hermes, Anubis, and the Valkyries.

Along with yews, boxwoods can be considered the psychopomps of the plant kingdom. Grave goods in Egyptian tombs were made or embellished with the wood of the boxwood plant. In Britain, Ireland, and France right up to the 1800s, sprigs were often provided to funeral-goers to toss into the grave of a loved one as a symbol of everlasting life in the hereafter. If you have ever wondered why you often see boxwoods planted around cemeteries, there's your answer.

CRAFTING: Runes

Given this association with the spirits or ancestors in the afterlife, it makes sense that boxwood is an excellent material from which to make runes. Boxwood has a dense yet easy-to-carve character that has made it popular with woodworkers for thousands of years.

Ideally, this work would be done in a waning moon. You will need roughly 24 to 28 inches of boxwood stems about the diameter of your forefinger. Carefully whittle away the thin outer bark. Removing the bark on a long stem is much easier than trying to get it off of small bits. Set the stems in a place to dry, if the wood has not already dried. This can take up to 2 months in a warm, dry place.

Once the wood has dried, cut it into discs. This will require a fine-tooth saw, either a hand tool or an electric Dremel-type tool. Fortunately, given its fine texture, box-wood requires very little sanding. You can use a boxcutter or carving tool to etch out the rune symbols in the discs, or you can use a wood-burning tool to make the marks. If you like, the discs can be varnished when completed. You can just as easily polish your rune set with tung oil to preserve your work.

When your work is completed, it would be proper to cleanse your runes at ritual and dedicate them to an appropriate chthonic deity or to your patron.

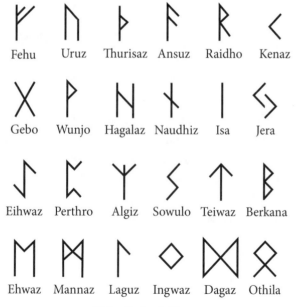

Elder Futhark Runes

CHERRY

Latin Name: *Prunus*

Locations: Landscapes, orchards, forests

Parts Used: Leaf, pit, berry, and sap

Hardiness Zones: 5 to 7

Planetary Ruler: Venus

Uses: For love spells, poppets, and lust; cherry juice is used for ink; congealed tree sap is used as a substitute for brains in spells calling for them.

Edibility: Berries are edible.

Warning: The leaves, twigs, and bark of this plant have some medicinal uses but only under the guidance of a professional. Cherry pits are toxic.

For all things related to love, no plant comes more readily to mind than cherry—except maybe roses. We make use of all parts of the plant for this purpose.

Appearance

Cherry, or *Prunus*, is found both in the wild and in the landscape and grows 20 to 30 feet in height. It blooms white in the woods and typically pink or white in the landscape. Many homes have either a Kwanzan (*P. serrulata* 'Kwanzan'), Higan (*P. subhirtella*), or Yoshino (*Prunus ×yedoensis*) cherry somewhere nearby.

Wild black cherry trees in North America (*P. serotina*) can be found as understory trees in most of the United States east of the Mississippi River. Chokecherry (*P. virginiana*) is generally found in the northern tier states. Both have a cluster of small white flowers in the spring. These will be followed by a dark, shiny fruit about the size of a pea. Unless it is flowering, you probably won't notice it in the forest.

Beyond the flowers, cherry trees are nondescript. They have oval, grass-green leaves. The bark is generally brown, gray, or light black. If you look closely, you will see horizontal scoring marks on the trunk. This isn't bug or animal damage. It's a natural habit of the tree.

The only other "flag" to help you spot a cherry tree in the wild that I know of is to watch in spring for tent worms. These caterpillars hide in massive, thick webs and they absolutely love wild cherry trees. They weave great globs of these tents among the tree branches near a fork in the tree. Spring tent worms won't hurt you, but they can defoliate a tree in years when the population spikes.

History

In the landscape, people tend to plant ornamental cherries. Fruiting trees are either ornamental, in that they don't make a usable fruit, or they are orchard trees with a fruit big enough to be usable in the home or marketplace. Cherry trees have always been popular in landscapes but interest in them really took off when in 1912 the mayor of Tokyo gifted over 3,000 cherry trees to the people of the United States as a gesture of friendship. Landscape cherry trees make an insignificant fruit that you may or may not notice. If you look, some years you may see a few berries; other years you won't. When they appear, birds love the berries; humans not so much so. The easiest way to spot a cherry tree in the landscape is to watch for it to bloom sometime between March and May. Yoshinos, the trees often associated with the Cherry Blossom Festival in Washington, DC, bloom earliest. Kwanzan tends to close out the season with the latest blooms.

Uses

Cherry is a Venus herb, and so the bark is good for love spells. Try to gather bark from trees that have already been cut, if that is what you need for your spell. Peeling bark from a living tree is relatively easy to do on a cherry but it will be very detrimental to the plant. Fruit trees of all sort live a very short life compared to their cousins in the forest. If you score the bark, the plant will "bleed," or ooze sap. Sap is largely sugar water. The damage attracts all manner of insects and disease. You could unintentionally be condemning a tree to an early death by tapping it.

That said, a walk through the woods will invariably lead you to a cherry tree that has been damaged naturally. Maybe a deer was rubbing his antlers on it. Maybe a careless ATV driver careened off of it. Whatever the cause, damage to the tree bark will cause the plant to ooze a golden sap that tends to harden into a dirty dark brown resin. Removing the resin for magickal work won't harm the tree; it will simply continue to ooze until the damaged area is, hopefully, hardened off. The sap can be used in spells to cause headaches or problems for others

Gather the spring flowers for a luscious love bath. Gathering the blossoms can be a bit of a challenge, however. Cherry blossoms are very fragile and tend to fade quickly. One easy way to catch them is to spread a sheet or a tarp under the tree as soon as you see it begin to bloom. Keep an eye on it to bring the material in if rain or frozen precipitation threatens.

The best blossoms to gather are from the Kwanzan cherry tree. While I'm told the Japanese consider these large, double blossoms gaudy, Americans love them. They truly look like the tissue flowers you may have made in elementary school, only in miniature. Plus, since Kwanzan trees bloom in late April to early May, you stand less of a chance of losing your harvest to a late-season snowstorm.

The cherry pit can be used as a talisman for love. The pit is used as the heart in poppets. The fruit itself can be used to make a love ink. I explain a little more about how to make inks on page 223 when I talk about pokeweed. If you don't have a source of cherry fruit around your area, there is nothing wrong with "harvesting" your fruit at the grocery store when they come in season there. Whether you are using the store-bought cherries for the pits or for ink, simply physically cleanse the fruit before your work.

CRAFTING: Cherry Jam

Before I leave the discussion on cherries, it is worth noting a recipe provided by Nostradamus himself. Yes, it turns out Nostradamus was not only a seer who left us prophecies covering thousands of years, he was also a bit of a spellworker. Actually, he seems to have called himself (quite legitimately) an apothecary. He did study for eight years to become one. However, that didn't stop him from making love spells, potions for beauty as well as health, and even kitchen recipes. He wrote it all down in his book entitled *Traité des fardements et confitures (Treatise on Cosmetics and Jams)*.

Nostradamus provides a recipe for cherry jam that he assures us is fit for a king and has a "taste to such an extent that, if a sick person takes just a single one, it will be to him like a balsam or other restorative." He also advocated for the use of cherries to improve psychic visions.[31]

Nostradamus tells us to boil 1½ pounds of sugar in the juice of 3 to 4 pounds of the best cherries we can find. It is worth noting that in some translations, Nostradamus advises that the sugar and whole cherries (pits, stems and all) are worked prior to boiling by the preparer. He or she must crush the berries and sugar together by hand in a mash while focusing on his or her intent—that is, the concoction of a mixture that will be life giving and will aid in psychic ability.

If any scum forms on the top of the juice as it boils, skim it off. Boil for roughly 20 minutes. If you are working with

---

31. Dennis W. Hauck, *Sorcerer's Stone: A Beginner's Guide to Alchemy* (New York: Citadel Press, 2004), 65.

raw cherries and not just cherry juice, strain the mixture to remove the skins and pits. Return the juice to a boil. Have ready 3 more pounds of cherries that have been pitted and the stems removed. Add the extra cherries to the boiling liquid.

Return the mixture to a boil, again removing any scum that forms. The jam is ready when you can drop a spoonful onto a plate and see that it holds a soft mound shape. Nostradamus advised putting the mixture up in 4-ounce containers that can be securely sealed. The dosage is 1 tablespoon daily, whether your goal is good health or stronger visions.

CHICKWEED

Latin Name: Stellaria media

Locations: Lawns, waste areas

Parts Used: Entire plant

Hardiness Zones: 3 to 8

Planetary Ruler: Moon

Uses: For love spells, lunar magick, and bird magick

Edibility: The entire plant is edible.

Warning: None

In today's society, chickweed is a weed. It's frequently found in the lawn in spring and fall. It's Latin name is *Stellaria media* because of the tiny little star-like flowers it produces. Because other low-growing, cool-season annuals can look a lot like chickweed, you should look closely at the plant before you harvest.

Appearance

Chickweed grows in a low mound. The first flush of bright green color in the dead of winter could very well be chickweed. The leaves will be hairless, stemless, and rounded to slightly oval in shape. You should see a thin line of plant hairs on the major stalk from which the leaves grow.

Those star-shaped flowers have five petals that end with a slight split. The flowers are borne in clusters as the plant matures. The entire top of the plant is used in magick.

The plant crops up in lawns, shrub borders, and flower beds. Though it's such a delicate-looking plant on first emerging in the spring, chickweed can quickly overwhelm the area where it is growing. I've seen single plants easily reach 18 inches across. It is boosted in its habit by a sturdy taproot and by its ability to develop little roots at each node along its branches.

History

Chickweed is naturalized all over the Northern Hemisphere. It has been used as a food crop for humans since the time of the ancient Greek civilizations and, as you might have guessed from the name, for poultry. Unlike some of the green plants people used to eat just to stay alive, chickweed is actually pretty good for you. It is comparable to spinach in vitamin and mineral content.

Because of its watery content, it is cooling and soothing when applied to irritated skin. Additionally, you will sometimes see chickweed included in herbal weight loss teas because it is a gentle diuretic.

Uses

Chickweed is a moon herb, as you might have guessed by its very watery nature. Chickweed is good for lunar magick as well as for spells to attract or keep a lover. It can also be used in beauty spells.

CRAFTING: Glamoury Water

Chickweed is also a bit of a glamoury herb. You can use it in love magick to give that dewy look of youth and vitality. It is actually used in naturopathy to soothe skin rashes. It can be taken internally as a tea to help flush toxins and excess water from the body.

To make a chickweed glamoury water, gather the herb during a waxing moon. Be sure to take it from a spot that you are sure has not been treated with herbicides or other chemicals. You can pull the entire plant, but as mentioned earlier, chickweed tends to root as it runs. When you pull it up, you may also get a lot of organic material that you will then need to clean away.

A better approach is to use scissors to cut about 2 cups of the top away. Wash the plant material in fresh water. Pat it dry and then spread it out to allow it to wilt for 1 to 2 days. Put the wilted material in a glass pint jar and fill with pure water. If your drinking water is treated, don't use tap water. Buy a bottle of spring water and fill the jar.

Set the jar in the moonlight outside if possible or in a window where the light can hit it if temperatures are too cold to leave the jar outside. Remove it from the window the next morning. That evening, set up your altar according to your tradition. Burn incense that will be pleasing to the deity of your tradition whose energies are aligned with love and beauty. Most love deities will be perfectly happy with rose or jasmine. But some, like Erzulie, might like to have a little cinnamon spice as well.

The candles to use during this working are white, red, pink, or a combination of these colors. Focus your meditation on your intent as you ask for help in blessing your moon water. Hold that intention for as long as you can. When you can't hold your focus any longer, thank the deity for his or her help. Let the candles and incense burn out in a safe manner.

When the candles are out, take your moon water and strain the herb out through cheesecloth or a coffee filter. Give it a good squeeze to get as much of the water as possible. You should be left with between 8 and 12 ounces. Fill the rest of the jar up with unflavored vodka. You can add a few drops of cinnamon or rose essential oil if you like. Store in the refrigerator until needed. Use it as a facial toner when you are out for a romantic evening or even when you need to "put your best face forward" in a sales meeting or business venture.

CHICORY

Latin Name: Cichorium intybus

Locations: Dry, gravelly areas

Parts Used: Root

Hardiness Zones: 2 to 9

Planetary Ruler: Sun or Venus

Uses: Removing obstacles, cursing, and to gain favors

Edibility: All parts are edible.

Warnings: None

Chicory has dusty blue flowers on a coarse plant that seems to like roadsides and old parking lots. Perhaps that is where it gets its reputation for promoting frugality in life. In bad times, people used the root as a coffee substitute, and the root is what is used in magick. It blooms all summer long. You may occasionally see it referred to in grimoires as "succory."

Appearance

The plant is perennial and can range in size from 10 to 40 inches tall with a spread of roughly 24 to 30 inches, depending on growing conditions. The leaves are long and narrow with a ragged edge. Chicory has a taproot that is as tenacious as that of dandelion. It grabs on to a location and holds on for dear life. Keep that in mind if you plan to dig a chicory plant up.

The flowers appear in early summer and come throughout the rest of the season. Because the plant is in the Asteraceae family, the shape is like a daisy flower. In fact, it is sometimes called blue daisy.

It is also sometimes called cornflower, but don't be mislead. The true cornflower is *Centaurea cyanus*—different type of plant (biennial), different growing season (spring), different plant shape—let's just say, they aren't the same thing and aren't used interchangeably.

History

The leaves of chicory are eaten as a salad green, although they are bitter in flavor. In fact, certain cultivated types of chicory turn up in the salad bar quite frequently in the form of endive lettuce and radicchio. The root of *C. intybus* var. *sativum* (European chicory) is roasted and added to coffee or used as a coffee substitute. If you have ever had Community brand coffee, you've had a blend of dark roast coffee and European chicory. You can find Community coffee in most well-stocked grocery stores or online, but it is best enjoyed in New Orleans while relaxing at a street café and soaking in the ambience of the city, in my opinion.

Uses

Chicory is sometimes ascribed to the sun. In fact, ancient writers such as Thessalus, Pliny, and Dioscorides say it is proper to rub your body with the juice of the chicory plant when invoking Helios (Phoebus).[32] But in Greek, Roman, and European folklore, the plant is often linked to love—either love lost or love aspired to. There is your Venus association.

Helios, in one myth, was said to have rejected a Oceanid named Clytie. She pined away for him in vain on the side of a road, her face following his track across the sky. Finally, she rooted in place, her body becoming a plant and her face becoming a flower. Old sources call the resulting flower "heliotrope," but translations in context indicate it was, in fact, chicory.

Young girls in Rome were encouraged to dig up the chicory root using a gold blade or the horn of a stag (associations with the sun) and carry the root on their person to keep a lover faithful and enamoured of their best qualities. This could be where the root gets its attributes of removing obstacles and gaining favors in general. Carrying the root has been extrapolated over the years to help anyone gain favor with a boss, a law officer, or judge or in any negotiation.

CRAFTING: Talisman Magick

Folklorist Robert Folkard recorded in his 1912 book *Plant Lore, Legend, and Lyrics* that chicory root "breaks all bonds, removes thorns from the flesh, and even renders the owner

32. J. H. M. Strubbe, "'Cursed be he that moves my bones,'" in *Magika Hiera*, 56.

invisible."[33] This might be a good time to remind folks that you can't take the old spells too literally. Chicory root will not make you fade from view as though you had just put on an invisibility cloak. In this case, it can at best make you less noticeable.

The magick in the herb in this case is the tangible reminder of your intent, similar to the use of a sigil. A sigil in magick is a symbol that imbodies your intent. Consider it a type of shorthand. By creating a sigil that is unique to your purpose, you create an object to focus on that will allow you to concentrate on the intent of your magick, not all the reason, rationale, and mechanics behind that intent.

In this case, you can make a mojo bag with chicory and, if you like, an equal amount of poppy seed, another herb for invisibility. Add to the bag a piece of smoky quartz and bloodstone. I would also add a piece of carnelian or garnet for courage. I find that often, if one needs to shield oneself from a situation or person, one also needs the courage to actually take that first step and follow through.

I find that sometimes, people assume once the bag is assembled, their work is done. This kind of magick needs to be reinforced regularly. This can be done during your daily meditation. If you don't do a daily meditation, set aside time either first thing in the morning upon rising or just before you go to bed to charge your mojo bag. Hold the bag and see yourself going about your life calmly, qui-

33. Robert Folkard, *Plant Lore, Legends, and Lyrics* (London: R. Folkard and Son, 1884), 304.

etly, wrapped in a soft gray fog. Breath deeply and ask for protection from the deity or deities with whom you work. Whether you need to be unseen by an annoying person, an authority figure, or a boss on the rampage, see yourself carrying on your life without interference from these annoyances. After completing your meditation, make sure you take steps in the mundance world to reinforce your intent.

Don't engage in bad behavior. Don't hang around locations where you know that annoying person is bound to be. By all means, if you are trying to avoid an abusive person, get yourself away from that person and alert appropriate authorities if your life or health is in danger.

Carry your talisman with you at all times and recharge it daily. The chicory root and crystals are tangible reminders of your intent. Carried in your pocket or in a gris-gris bag or even in a little witch's bottle hung around your neck, it is your solid reminder in the workplace to keep your mouth shut, stay away from toxic people, and just do your job—in other words, to remain invisible in plain sight.

CLOVER

Latin Name: *Trifolium*

Locations: Lawns, fields, roadsides

Parts Used: Leaf

Hardiness Zones: 3 to 10

Planetary Ruler: Mercury

Uses: Protection, money, and good luck

Edibility: Edible

Warning: None

Clover. Lucky clover! I've already talked about it to a limited degree. It pops in many lawns, much to the homeowner's dispair! It is a good example of how color can influence the use of a plant. White clover (*Trifolium repens*) flowers are said to protect against negative magick. Red clover (*T. pratense*) flowers aid in financial matters and love. All clover is good for luck, although many focus on the four-leaf clover for that purpose.

Appearance

In the old books, what is called clover is often refered to as "trefoil"—basically meaning three leaves. Another name for the plant hundreds of years ago was "three-leave grass." If you look about in the landscape or on the roadside for a plant with three leaves clustered in the form of a club as depicted on a playing card, you'll find plenty of candidates, including several varieties of shamrock (*Oxalis regnellii*), ornamental oxalis such as *O. triangularis,* and wood sorrel (*O. acetosella*).

But shamrocks are not clovers. An easy way to tell a shamrock or oxalis from a clover is to look at the leaf markings. On all clovers, you should find a white crescent lightly marked on each of its three leaves. The markings on oxalis, when they are there, are splotches of black, brown, and in some cases burgundy.

Another way to identify the plant is to look at it in bloom. Oxalis species bloom with a five-petaled flower in either yellow, pink, rose, or white. What is called shamrock blooms in spring and eventually fades back in the fall until it goes completely dormant. The wild oxalis, or wood sorrel, blooms off and on throughout the season.

True clovers make a globe flower with tubular petals. Bees love clover, which is unfortunate if you happen to be allergic to bee stings but great if you like clover-flavored honey. The plant flowers most abundantly in spring but will also throw up flowers throughout the summer.

History

While modern homeowners curse the clover growing in their lawns, it is interesting to note that the plant was once considered a staple ingredient in all lawn seed mixtures. Clover grows in almost any condition and climate. It doesn't die back in the winter except in the most harsh climates. Plus, it improves the soil.

Modern tastes have changed, however, as well as concerns about bee stings in an era when many people suffer from allergic reactions.

While it is still used in certain farming applications, clover is more esteemed now for its medicinal uses.

Uses

Clover is a good plant to use in spells for prosperity and love. These two attributes are enshrined in our language, as when people say, "We're in the clover" and "Roll me over in the clover." The first is a farming reference to livestock happily feeding on fields of clover, getting fat and sassy in the process. Healthy livestock mean prosperity to the folks who raised them. Early farmers may not have known about the science behind plant growth, but those fields of clover were performing another bit of magick below ground. Clover is a nitrogen-fixing plant. With the help of a special bacteria, clover draws nitrogen from the air. In its root system (and again with help from the bacteria) the nitrogen is converted to a form plants can use and animals can digest. Clover actually creates something from nothing, in a sense. That is truly a magickal form of prosperity.

As for the other association for clover, that of "Roll me over in the clover," that is quite frankly a reference to sex. It's more of a European thing, as I understand it. Americans would be more inclined to say "a romp in the hay." Regardless, red clover in particular is associated with attracting a lover and keeping him or her.

You can do as our forefathers and foremothers did and carry a clover leaf over your heart to attract a companion. Perhaps you would like to secure a clover leaf over the door to your residence. Allegedly, this would draw a companion to your home. You can take a romance bath using red or pink candles instead of the green ones called for in the magickal bath spell that follows. In this case, the focus of your meditation should be on the qualities you desire in a companion, not a fixed image of a particular person. That would be baneful magick—not a good idea.

CRAFTING: Prosperity Wash and Spell

You can tap this herb's energy by using it in a prosperity wash or bath during a waxing moon in the sign of Mercury. Gather a cup of clover, in bloom if possible. Some sources recommend using red clover; others say white is okay. White clover has the added association of protecting us from bad people and events. Prepare a comfortable bath and add the clover to the bath water. If you are able, create the right atmosphere by bathing by the light of green candles.

As you relax in the bath, focus on your monetary goals. Don't concentrate on winning the lottery or waking up to find a bag of money at the foot of your bed. Focus on seeing a resolution to your money problems. When I do prosperity spells, I like to visualize my checkbook with a high balance, five figures or more, in the ledger. See yourself literally swimming in money. Feel the satisfaction that comes with having your bills paid plus a little left over for the things you want in life. When you can no longer keep the imagery in your mind, get out of the tub. See your money problems flowing away as the tub drains. Respectfully discard the plant material in the compost pile or running water or bury it in the ground.

The magick in this and other prosperity spells is to set yourself up to succeed. You should be doing those things in the mundane world that help create prosperity too, such as speaking up for that raise at work, keeping an ear to the ground for better employment possibilities, and not spending your income on frivolous pursuits. Magick lines the universe up to help us achieve our goals. It is up to us to see and take advantage of those goals.

CLUB MOSS

Latin Name: Lycopodium

Locations: Forest floors

Parts Used: Entire plant

Hardiness Zones: 3 to 8

Planetary Ruler: Moon

Uses: Protection, power, and purification

Edibility: Some medicinal uses but considered inedible

Warning: The spores of club moss are nontoxic but
   flammable.

The most common form of club moss in my area is running
cedar. In another example of those name changes we mentioned
earlier, running cedar used to be known as *Lycopodium digitatum*.
Now it is categorized as *Diphasiastrum digitatum* but it is still in

the Lycopodiaceae family. Other names for plants in this group are fan club moss, crow's foot, and bear's paw. You may have to search a bit for this one. Another moon herb, it likes wooded areas that stay cool, moist, and well-drained.

Appearance

To identify fan club moss in the wild, look for a stiff, dull green plant that runs and roots along the top of the ground in the loose forest compost. It is especially fond of acidic soils. Look for it in pine forests or tree stands dominated by nut trees (oak, pecan, hickory, etc.). Its common name of running cedar comes from the observation that it looks like someone laid a cedar branch on the ground. The club moss moniker is related to the club shape of the spore stem and the mossy look of the plant.

History

Club mosses are among some of the oldest plants in the plant kingdom, evolving roughly 410 million years ago. They have been used by humans for dyes, medicine, skin treatments, and even as a coating for pills at one time. The spores have a high oil content. These were sometimes used to aid in ceremonial displays, as the leader of the ceremony would throw some spores in the fire at just the right time to achieve a bright flash of light.[34] When photography was in its infancy, club moss spores were used to provide the flash in flash photography.

---

34. Marion Lobstein, "Clubmosses: An Ancient and Interesting Group of 'Fern Allies,'" Prince William Wildflower Plant Society, accessed September 30, 2020, https://vnps.org/princewilliamwildflowersociety /botanizing-with-marion/clubmosses-an-ancient-and-interesting-group -of-fern-allies/.

At one time, this was considered an endangered plant. As I write this, the running cedar plant population has recovered. However, other *Lycopodium* species growing throughout the country have not.

I said before that plants among the same family can be interchanged. I can use white oak or live oak interchangeably for magickal workings. Technically, that would be true of plants in the *Lycopodium* genus. But if one or more of the species are endangered and that is all you can find in your area, leave it alone. Pagans have plenty of options for different plants that can be used for every need imaginable. Select something that will not contribute to the decline of its species.

There is one more option. While this book is about helping you find plants growing naturally and freely in and around your home, it can also lead you to cultivated varieties. Scarsely a plant in the wild exists that hasn't been cultivated or hybridized for use on the farm or in the garden. The same is true of club moss.

If you would like to grow your own, *Selaginella kraussiana,* or African club moss, is available as a houseplant in most areas of the United States. It is especially good for use in those popular fairy gardens I see a lot of people creating or buying. The moist growing environment of a terrarium is perfect for club moss. I realize quite a few fairy gardens are more dish garden than terrarium, but the environment is basically the same—low to moderate light, damp growing conditions, and cramped root zones with plants huddled closely together. Add some pretty, shiny baubles and you have the perfect way to honor the Fae right in your own home.

With all that said, running cedar gives me an opportunity to mention something else about the plant kingdom. Seeing the interconnectedness of the plant kingdom can be difficult. I know, as Pagans, we are supposed to be more in tune with the notion that all life is connected on a World Web. Unfortunately, it doesn't often smack us in the face.

My mother loved running cedar. She tried many times to move sets closer to the house. It never worked. First, running cedars grow very, very slowly. It can take twenty years for a *Lycopodium* to mature from spore to plant. Second, you can't just move the plant. Running cedar is one of those plants that has a symbotic relationship with particular fungi that are present in the soil. If you don't have the fungi, running cedar won't grow. You can't see fungi (as a general rule) so, how could Mama have known?

We are all connected, often in ways we don't understand. Perhaps we will never know, in certain cases. Learn as much as you can about the plants you hope to use to help you in your path. Do no harm, to the best of your ability.

Uses

W. Winwood Reade wrote a book titled *The Veil of Isis, or The Mystery of the Druids* in 1861. In book 3, chapter 7, he describes how club moss was gathered ritually by a virgin who was then purified with it to become a personification of the moon.[35] From examples like this, you can see that you can use club moss for protection and purification. Any part of the plant is collected for spellwork. Using it during esbats or for honoring a lunar deity would also be appropriate.

---

35. W. Winwood Reade, *The Veil of Isis, or The Mysteries of the Druids,* bk. 3 (London: Charles J. Skeet, 1861), ch. 7.

CRAFTING: Cleansing Magickal Wash

You can make a club moss wash to clean your goddess statues, cauldron, stones related to the moon, and any of your magickal tools. First, gather some rain water during a waxing moon. If you don't have the right setting to do this, try to find some clean running water from a river or stream. In a pinch, run some tap water and set it out in a crystal bowl to absorb the moon's energy as it is waxing. Bring it in the next morning before the sun is high in the sky.

Gather your club moss, respectfully, and on the next night, add the herb to your moon water. Let this sit outside overnight. If you can't leave it outside, try to find a window that catches the moonlight and set your water there. The next morning, strain the water. You can dry the club moss for use again later, or you can compost it to give it back to the earth.

That night or any night before the moon begins to wane, set up a work area outside if possible. You don't have to set up an altar but you can. Bring the items you plan to clean outside and gently wash them in the moon water while she is high overhead. You can sing any songs used in your tradition as you work. You can meditate on your connection to the Divine Feminine. Or you can simply say your adorations to the lunar goddesses you revere.

Once the items are cleansed, leave them sitting outside to air dry under the light of the moon if possible. Gather them in the next morning before the sun gets high in the sky and enjoy their gentle radiant energy.

DAISY

Latin Name: Bellis perennis, Leucanthemum vulgare

Locations: Fields, ditches, flower gardens

Parts Used: Flower

Hardiness Zones: 4 to 9

Planetary Ruler: Venus

Uses: Love, friendship, and fairy magick

Edibility: L. vulgare is edible.

Warning: The leaves and flowers of B. perennis are
mildly toxic.

Mention daisy and everyone seems to know what you are
talking about. The word has become more of an adjective than a
noun. I've done it myself on an earlier page in this book at least

once. Do you recall when I talked about chicory with a shape "like a daisy flower"?

So many plants are described as "daisy-like," meaning a flower that has a distinct disc, usually yellow, around which are arranged numerous petals. The petals of daisy-like flowers come in all of the colors of the rainbow. After all, the daisy is lumped into a plant family that has roughly 23,600 relatives.

Appearance

To be a true daisy, the plants you want are *Leucanthemum vulgare* (formerly listed as *Chrysanthemum leucanthemum*) and *Bellis perennis*. Both have a raised, yellow disc and many petals radiating out from that disc. Oddly, this white-rayed flower with the yellow eye is not considered a sun herb. It is ruled by Venus. When the ancients writers such as Discorides developed the doctrine of signatures, they said that the daisy reminded them of the moon.

The field daisies or ox-eyed daisies that grow on the side of the road and at the edges of fields hold their flower heads high in May and June. The foliage is dark green with rounded edges or scallops. The lower parts of the flower stem are hairy; the upper parts, not so much so. The most popular cultivated field daisy is the Shasta daisy that often shows up in bouquets from the florist.

History

Daisy is the flower of youth and innocence. Little children with flowers in their hair come to mind when this flower is mentioned. It was the very emblem of the flower child of the 1960s hippie culture. The naivete of youth was immortalized with pictures of young people putting daisies into the gun barrels of law enforcement officers in a march on Washington, DC, to protest America's involvement in Vietnam during that era.

When I say that daisy is another herb that is used for love, I don't mean lusty love. I mean love that is pure and without condition. I mean love that is fresh and tender. If you want sex, you go with roses. If you want a *Romeo and Juliet* type of love, you use daisies.

The great American botanist Luther Burbank loved the field daisies he knew as a child. As an adult, he worked at making a larger-flowering version of his childhood daisy using *L. vulgare* and *L. maximum*. He crossed that offspring with *L. lacustre*. The result of that was crossed with *Nipponanthemum nipponicum*, the Japanese daisy. After much patience and many trials, he came up with the Shasta daisy in 1901, a mainstay in many perennial gardens today.

Uses

Because daisy is governed by Venus, you can use the flower petals in any spells relating to her. That makes the flower perfect for moon rituals or for honoring any deity associated with the moon.

Daisy is used in love divination (He loves me, he loves me not). Or you can sleep with a daisy root under your pillow to draw your love back to you. Fairies are fond of daisies. A good way to pander to them is to set up a special altar for them at Beltane and Midsummer that features plenty of daisies.

CRAFTING: Moon Ritual

Pagans in some traditions honor moon deities at the esbat ritual. *Esbat* is based on a French word that means "wild frolic," but you don't have to work up a frenzy to hold an esbat ritual. I like to use the time of the full moon to simply connect with Mother Goddess and thank her for being in my life. The ritual can be as complex or as straightforward as you like.

Hopefully, you can do this ritual outside under the light of the moon. If not, try to find a window through which you can see the moon. Set your ritual area up according to your custom. Decorate it with daisies around a white candle. I like to focus on the moon as it drifts past the tree branches. That might not be comfortable for some. Another way to scry at the moon is to do so with a bowl of water.

Float some daisies in the water. After you have welcomed the Divine Feminine to your ritual area, stand with your back to the moon but in such a way as to allow the reflection of the moon in the water to be seen. Focus on the image as you let your mind go still. If you are not confident that you can keep your mind still, focus on the moon deity you have invited to your ritual. See her in your mind's eye. How do her hair, her eyes, and her clothing appear? How does she greet you?

In my experience, deity rarely speaks. Most often we are given images or strong feelings that require consideration after the ritual is over. When she is gone, thank her for her presence even if you didn't receive a message. The experience is enough. Close the ritual and ground according to your tradition.

You can strain and store your moon water for future use. You can use it to bless your houseplants. Discard the spent flowers respectfully by tossing them into a running stream or the compost bin or by burying them in the ground or under landscape mulch in a shrub border.

DANDELION

Latin Name: Taraxacum officinale

Locations: Lawns, roadsides

Parts Used: Seed head, leaf, root

Hardiness Zones: 3 to 9

Planetary Ruler: Jupiter

Uses: Love divination, calling spirits, strength, health, and psychic powers

Edibility: All parts are edible.

Warning: None

Who hasn't wished upon a dandelion puffball? Dandelions tend to be evergreen, always around, but they bloom the best in late spring and early summer. Some sources say it is a sun herb, probably because of its bright yellow flower. In fact, one old source gives the word *sonnenwirbel,* meaning "sun vortex," as one of the German words for dandelion.[36] It is, perhaps, a reference to either the summer solstice or the general power of the sun.

Then again, others say dandelion is ruled by Jupiter. Either way, it has a masculine energy.

Appearance

Because it is so recognizable in the landscape, I hardly need to describe this perennial plant. Dandelion grows from a rosette of leaves attached to a sturdy taproot. The leaf looks like someone took lance-shaped foliage and rapidly tore jagged edges into it. The ragged shape of the leaf is famously thought to be the origin of the word *dandelion,* which comes from French, *dent de lion,* based on the Latin *dens liones,* meaning "lion's tooth."

In spring and sporadically throughout the year, it casts a bright yellow flower with strap-like petals. The flower gives way to a rounded globe of seeds that float away on the wind to set even more plants.

A few plants exist that look somewhat like dandelion, such as hawkweed (*Hieracium*), but honestly, if you can't recognize dandelion, I seriously suspect you have been locked away from the great outdoors for most of your life.

History

The French don't call the flower dandelion; they call it *pissenlit,* or piss-in-bed, because of the plant's diuretic properties. For our purposes, dandelion is also known in parts of England as witch milk plant, a reference to the milk latex that oozes out when the

---

36. Folkard, *Plant Lore, Legends, and Lyrics,* 152.

leaf or stem is broken. The Scots are said to call it *witch's gowan* (marigold).

For people who take pride in their lawns, dandelion is a weed. It inspires frustration. You can't pull a dandelion out by the root in average soil. If even a bit of the root remains (and trust me, a bit will remain), the plant will regenerate. A bizarre tool exists primarily to help the gardener excise dandelions. You might be tempted to buy one for use in harvesting dandelion for magickal use. It looks like a screwdriver that someone filed to make a forked tip and then attached a metal loop to the shaft. The idea is you stick the forked tip into the ground beside the dandelion and then rock the tool back on the metal loop to pry the plant out of the ground. Don't waste your time or money. It doesn't work.

Uses

For herbalists, dandelion is a powerhouse of medicine. It is offered as a means to lose weight, control cholesterol, lower blood pressure, fight inflammation (inside and outside the body), and provide nutritional benefits to the diet. Primarly the root is used for medicinal purposes. Certain varieties of the plant are cultivated for these uses as well as for a coffee substitute (just like chicory). Surprisingly, when grown in good garden soil, the plant and the root can get quite large.

The fluffy seed head of dandelion makes this a popular divination herb. The number of things it can foretell are legion. Blow on the puffball and count the number of seeds left—that's how many years you will live. Blowing away all the seeds in one puff means your significant other loves you dearly. If some seeds remain, their love is in doubt. Blow on the puff head and watch which direction the seeds float. That is the direction in which your true love lies. Think of a message for a friend and blow it on the wind with the seeds of a dandelion.

I have come across many sources that suggest using a dandelion tea to enhance psychic abilities or to help achieve psychic dreams at night. Some say to use the leaves; others say use the root. The problem is dandelion is a Jupiter herb. Normally, Jupiter herbs aren't associated with psychic awareness or enhancement.

The same sources insist that dandelion is attributed to Hecate. Again, Hecate is not a sun goddess; she is most often associated with the moon. She does travel between worlds, so that would make her a viable source to consult when trying to scry. However, I would not use dandelion to try to contact her.

CRAFTING: Dandelion Infusion Recipe for Beltane

You can use dandelion in your rituals for Beltane. Gather enough dandelion flowers to fill a quart jar, making sure to pick from plants that have not been sprayed with pesticides. Remove any green part of the plant before brewing. Carefully pour boiling water over the flowers and allow them to steep until the liquid is cool. Strain the infusion through a cheesecloth. Flavor it to taste with honey and use it as part of the cakes and ale for your Beltane ritual.

Since Beltane marks the joining of the Divine Masculine and Divine Feminine energies, you can add sliced strawberries to the infusion to balance the masculine energy of dandelion with the feminine energy of the berries.

FERNS

Latin Name: *Polystichum, Osmunda, Nephrolepis,* and
  many more

Locations: Streamsides, homes

Parts Used: Leaf frond

Hardiness Zones: 3 to 10

Planetary Ruler: Mercury

Uses: Protection, concentration, weather magick, health,
  luck, and exorcism

Edibility: Only the fronds are edible.

Warning: The fiddleheads of most ferns are safe to eat
  but only after being cooked. However, all parts of
  bracken ferns (*Pteridium aquilinum*) are toxic.

Ferns come in many varieties in the wild, so you should be able to find some near you wherever you live in the United States. There are male ferns, lady ferns, Christmas ferns, cinammon ferns, hay ferns, holly ferns, and Japanese painted ferns. If that wasn't enough, you can find ferns indoors, such as Boston ferns, rabbit ferns, bird's nest ferns and on and on. But all are Mercury herbs.

It's hard to give you Latin names for ferns because there are so many. Some of the more popular ferns in the landscape are Christmas fern (*Polystichum acrostichoides*), male fern (*Dryopteris filix-mas*), cinnamon fern (*Osmundastrum cinnamomeum*), and Japanese painted ferns (*Athyrium niponicum*). I'm afraid I will have to say that all true ferns are in the Polypodiopsida class of plants and leave it to you to research what you have in your specific area.

Appearance

Basically, a fern is a plant that reproduces by spores instead of seeds. It has no flowers. The majority of ferns can be identified by the fronds or fiddlehead shape of the new foliage. Most ferns have what are called pinnate leaf structures. Pinnate is just a fancy way of saying leaflets or veins of a simple leaf "arranged as are the segments of a bird's feather, opposite or alternate from each other along a common axis, not radiating from one point."[37] But there are true ferns that have a broad leaf, such as the bird's nest fern (*Asplenium nidus*) and the staghorn fern (*Platycerium*).

Most plants have look-alikes and ferns are no exception. The popular houseplant asparagus fern (*Asparagus aethiopicus*) is not

---

37. Norman Taylor, ed., *Taylor's Encyclopedia of Gardening: Horticulture and Landscape Design,* 4th ed. (Boston, MA: Riverside Press, 1961), 917.

a true fern. A dead giveaway, if you can keep the plant alive long enough, is that asparagus ferns will flower and make a bright red berry. Remember, true ferns never flower or produce seeds, despite what some of the old grimores might tell you.

Outdoors, people sometimes confuse the fine-textured leaves of Queen Anne's lace (*Daucus carota*) or valerian (*Valeriana officinalis*) with that of ferns. Look closely and you will see these plants don't meet the standard of pinnate leaves with opposite leaflets along a single stem.

If this isn't confounding enough, air ferns not only aren't ferns, but they also aren't even plants. Air ferns are a cute little novelty item that people purchase when they are too busy to deal with a live plant. It looks like a vivid dark green, ferny brush and is usually stuck in a seashell or tiny decorative pot. What looks like a plant is really the dyed, dried-out skeletons of a species of marine animal called hydrozoan. Pretty to look at but not much use in your magickal work.

History

When I think of ferns, I always think of the great conservancy gardens like Kew Gardens in England. Many of these were constructed during the Victorian era when collections of tropical plants, including ferns, were popular. This encouraged people to set up their own little tiny terrariums, essentially miniature hothouses, to grow these exotic plants that previously could only be enjoyed in woodland settings.

Boston ferns (*Nephrolepis exaltata* 'Bostoniensis') were introduced in this era (1890) and became ubiquitous. They were loved for their rapid growth and fountain of fronds. Today in the summertime, you don't drive very far in any neighborhood without seeing several of these beauties decorating someone's front porch.

Uses

Ferns bring the rain and draw the Fae, especially pixies. In fact, witches who would like to work more closely with the Fae can plant a bed of ferns and dedicate it to this group of entities. To carry the spores of the bracken fern was to allow the holder to enter the realm of fairies. Being at peace with the Fae is a good idea. Most won't do you any serious harm if you tick them off, but they can make themselves a nuisance if they are unhappy with you.

As a brief aside, you might want to think twice about relying extensively on the Fae for your magickal workings. When most people think of fairies, they imagine the Victorian or Disney versions—light, happy little air elements who flit around the flowers bringing joy and happiness. Some do. Some don't.

The kingdom of the Fae includes a lot of different entities from pixies to kelpies. Not all of them think so fondly of humans. Fairies are not air elementals, but they do embody a lot of airlike qualities. They are invisible, changeable, and ephemeral in their focus. Fairies are not only the soft breeze of summer but the icy gust of winter. They can be easily offended or just plain indifferent to the needs of humans. I'm not saying don't reach out to them. I'm saying do so with caution.

Ferns repel evil spirits when burnt and protect the home when grown inside. Burning fern in an incense brings clarity and focuses the mind. Please take care if you use dried stalks of fern in a fire. They burn in a flash! As I said earlier, they are associated with fairies. They can be just as mercurial. If you are blending dried fern with other herbs, the risk is reduced.

Ferns were thought to be a natural enemy of cane plants (plants whose wood was used to make arrows) such that a poltice of fern roots was thought to be the best medicine to draw out arrows. In some of the African diaspora traditions, spreading dried ferns leaves along a windowsill is thought to keep burglars away.

CRAFTING: Glamoury Attraction Spell

Because of that association with fairies, ferns are a good ingredient to use in your glamoury or attraction spells. Glamoury magick is a way to ensure that your best qualities are seen first. It won't turn you into the latest runway model or celebrity, but it should enhance your finer traits.

I have made a simple ointment for a number of people, generally those in the marketing profession and occassionally those interested in landing a new job. On a Tuesday when the moon is in Mercury, gather and dry some fresh fern. Once dried, reduce it to a fine powder. You will need about a teaspoon of powdered fern.

Melt 2 tablespoons of either shea butter or cocoa butter over low heat or in the microwave. Add the fern to the melted butter along with 4 to 5 drops of neroli essential oil. You can also add 1 to 2 drops of vanilla, if you like. Blend well. Pour into a small container and allow to cool until it sets.

Before you go on your job interview or to meet a new client, light a gold or yellow candle and petition the Divine for help in your endeavor. You can speak with your patron deity (or deities), or you can call specifically to any of those involved with business and commerce, such as Mercury, Turms, Ekwensu, or Lugh. Before you shake hands with your interviewer or client, briskly rub some of the ointment into your hands. The herbs and oils will add to your powers of persuasion.

FLEABANE

Latin Name: *Erigeron philadelphicus*

Locations: Fields, roadsides

Parts Used: Leaves, flowers

Hardiness Zones: 2 to 8

Planetary Ruler: Moon

Uses: Exorcism and protection

Edibility: The leaves are edible.

Warning: None

Appearance

A European plant known as fleabane is *Pulicaria dysenterica,* syn. *Inula dysenterica.* It is a 2-foot-tall perennial with small yellow flowers that come in the fall and leaves that when crushed are said to smell like soap. I wouldn't know. This is a European native.

In North America, magickal practitioners turn to *Erigeron philadelphicus*, a white flower that blooms in the spring. Fleabane is common in abandoned fields, utility access areas, and road-sides. It is easy to spot in late winter when the light green foliage seems to "pop" against the faded leaves of winter. As the stems grow, you can see plenty of plant hairs along the stalk.

The plant is about 2 feet tall and bears clusters of daisy-like flowers. If you look closely at the flower head, you will notice the flower petals are almost threadlike. They are so thin, botanists call them ray florets, and you can see 10 to 20 of them in a cluster on a single plant.

The flower clusters are persistent when they begin to bloom around March, lingering for several weeks. As the flowers mature, they will begin to take on a pink tinge. When they fade, the dried flower heads look like lint. They tend to break apart and fly away easily. This makes the dried plant an excellent firestarter, a trait that the Lakota, Cherokee, and Navajo nations are said to have put to good use.[38]

History

Fleabane is another plant about which there can be some confusion in magickal resource books. Often, in the old magick books that were printed in Europe from 1200 to 1700 CE, a reference to fleabane was a reference to *I. dysenterica*.

In fact, in Donald Tyson's annotations for James Freake's translation for *Three Books of Occult Philosophy* by Cornelius

---

38. Geneve Bean, "Fleabane," The Herb Hound, last accessed June 28, 2020, http://theherbhound.blogspot.com/2016/09/fleabane.html.

Agrippa, Tyson specifically identifies Agrippa's use of fleabane seeds as *I. dysenterica*. When mixed with linseed, violet roots, and parsley and burned, the seeds would induce visions, according to Agrippa.[39]

Uses

Fleabane is variously attributed to the moon and to Venus. I think this might be due to the confusion between what is called fleabane in North America and the European fleabane. When ancient Greek sources such as Euripedes and Homer speak of fleabane, they associate it with the Greek god Hephaistos and the element of fire.

The priniciple use of fleabane is exorcism. But it can also be combined with St. John's wort for protection. Harold Roth of the website Alchemy Works writes of the legends that speak of Hephaistos when he bound Aries and Aphrodite in a trap to catch them in adulterous behavior. He was also said to have come between Zeus and his mother, Hera, when Zeus fell into to one of his fits of rage.[40] If you accept these ideas, it's easy to see where fleabane gets its correspondences.

CRAFTING: Exorcism Incense

Fleabane can be used to stuff poppets made to banish a problem or person. I use it most often in general exorcism incenses. I don't believe an incense has to smell rancid in order to banish. Sometimes you want that. Other times you just want an incense that is stronger than sage without

---

39. Agrippa, *Three Books of Occult Philosophy*, 129.
40. Harold A. Roth, "*Erigeron speciosus:* Showy Fleabane," accessed, June 29, 2020, alchemy-works.com/erigeron.html.

a lingering odor that makes you want to leave the house for a while.

I find an equal mix of copal, clove, and fleabane does the trick quite nicely. If you can't get or can't afford the copal, just use a balanced mix of clove and fleabane. It will work fine to either banish negativity or cleanse the ritual area after your working to ensure nothing bad hangs around.

GERANIUM

Latin Name: *Geranium maculatum*

Locations: Fields, roadsides, gardens

Parts Used: Root

Hardiness Zones: 3 to 11

Planetary Ruler: Venus

Uses: Peace, stability, confidence, spell breaking, binding, and harmony

Edibility: All parts of the plant are edible.

Warning: None

Remember when I wrote earlier in this book that knowing
the Latin names of the herbs you use comes in handy? Geranium
is a good example of why this advice is important.

I don't think there is any flower more readily identified with summer than geranium. But only if you are talking about *Pelargonium*. I'm not talking about *Pelargonium*; I am talking about the true geranium, *Geranium maculatum*, or cranesbill.

Appearance

Cranesbill can be bought in most garden centers and is a feature in cottage gardens. You will find wild geranium growing on the side of the road and in waste areas in the harshest of conditions. Our wild geranium has soft pink and white flowers on a small plant with deeply lobed leaves that are circular in form. The leaves can develop a red tint to the edges when the plant is under stress or as the season changes in fall. The hooked shape of its seeds gives this plant its common name, cranesbill.

The cultivated form is similar in shape but less prone to develop the red tinge to its leaves. The foliage is also deeper green and the form is more compact.

History

True geraniums were a favorite in European gardens for centuries before the arrival of *Pelargonium* from South Africa in the seventeenth century. Technically, the two plants were once classified together. Eventually, they were divided out into their own distinct categories. You will frequently see sources that tell you the two plants are interchangeable in magick. In my opinion, they are not. This is particularly true today. *Pelargonium* has been manipulated so thoroughly and completely that the ones you buy at the garden center have very little in common with their ancestors from South Africa. They have even less in common with their cousins, the true geranium.

To be clear, I have no problem growing and enjoying *Pelargonium*. All of that breeding and cross breeding has given us *Pelargonium* with wonderful fragrant leaves in addition to lovely flowers. I certainly have no problem using rose geranium (*P. graveolens*) oil in place of pure rose oil. The fragrance is a little less intense. Fortunately, so is the price!

Technically, European witches worked with *G. robertianum*, or herb Robert, also known as stinking Bob and, for some reason I have yet to discover, death-come-quickly. I've never actually smelled herb Robert. Perhaps it truly does smell that bad. When people from the Old World came to the New World, they discovered *G. maculatum* and found that it has much the same qualities—minus the bad smell.

Uses

Cranesbill root brings peace, stability, and harmony. Its reputation for protection was so strong that people used to carry a piece of the dried root in their pocket for safety when traveling.

Cranes were sometimes lumped together with storks, making this plant a good luck charm too. Romans were quite fond of storks, allowing the birds to build nests on their roofs because it was seen as an insurance policy for good fortune and a happy home.

For those of you who follow a Celtic path, this will be an especially significant herb. Cranes were sacred to the Celts, from the three cranes that guarded the home of Midhir to the bag made of crane skin that Mannanon mac Lir used to carry seven treasures. Modern Druids still use a symbolic crane bag to carry ritual tools and magickal items.

The Celts had a slightly different outlook on the nature of the luck that cranes could bring, however. The bird was considered to be bad luck. The Celts used this aspect of the bird to their advantage by embossing the bird's image on their weapons, using the bad luck to inflict harm to their enemies.

You might wonder how an herb mostly used for good luck and peace could also be used in binding magick. It helps to know that another name for cranesbill is alum root, owing to the astringent qualites of the plant that are similar to that of the mineral alum. Powdered cranesbill root was once kept on hand to be used on wounds to stop the bleeding.

Because of this quality, cranesbill can be used to bind a person or a situation. In some cases, in the old spells that have come down to us, cranesbill was used to bind a lover to a person. In other cases, it could be used to bind a person who was threatening to do harm, either to himself or to another.

CRAFTING: Binding Powder and Aerosol

If you need to do work to stop a gossiping coworker or associate, cranesbill should be a major ingredient in your working. When used for these purposes, it is best to gather the herb in a waning moon on a Saturday, if possible.

You have two options to create a usable magickal tool. The most discrete is to make an aerosol; the second option is to make a fine powder.

You will need at least ½ ounce of material. Gather the root when the moon begins to wane and dry it using one of the methods discussed in chapter 5. Chop the root, all the time thinking of your intent to stop your associate from spreading rumors or gossip about you. Put the material in a small jar along with a few lumps of dragon's blood resin, if you have it. Seal the jar and allow it to set—ideally for 1 lunar cycle but at least for 1 week. After the time has passed, strain the liquid and transfer it to a small spray bottle.

If you prefer to make a powder, take the dried root and grind it to dust. This will take some doing, even if you are using an electric grinder. If you are using a mortar and pestle, this is a great opportunity to take your frustration with this associate out on the material. When it is finely ground, add to the powder some finely ground dragon's blood resin. Put the powder in a plastic bag or container where it will stay dry.

At this point, whether you are using spray or powder, on a Saturday during the waning moon, set up your altar according to your tradition. Use a black candle. You can burn powdered cranesbill root as an incense or dragon's blood incense. Meditate on the source of your problem as you hold the spray bottle or packaged powder in your hands. Visualize that person with his or her mouth puckering up every time he or she tries to speak against you. You can also see this person with a wide band of tape over his or her mouth. Hold the image as long as you can. When you can no longer do that, allow the candle and incense to burn out.

This material can be sprayed on the person's door or sprinkled at the doorway. If you don't have access to the person's home, it can be used in the workplace when you won't be seen doing the application. Spray the liquid on the person's work chair or work station or sprinkle the powder on the carpet around their station. Give the working 1 lunar cycle to have an effect. When it does have an effect, be sure to light a candle and thank your deities or the universe in general for helping clear this problem from your life.

GRASS

Latin Name: Poaceae

Locations: Lawns, roadsides, fields

Parts Used: Leaf

Hardiness Zones: 1 to 12

Planetary Ruler: Varies

Uses: Psychic powers, protection

Edibility: Grasses are nontoxic but generally not eaten.

Warning: Grasses may cause contact dermatitis in some
  people.

When it comes to grass for magickal working, we open a can of Poaceae (plant family name of all grasses). What are Pagans talking about when a spell or ritual calls for grass? Wild stands of grass cover over 41 percent of the world. Rice is a grass. Corn is a grass. Bamboo is a grass. Lemongrass is a grass. And, yes, that stuff growing in the lawn in front of your residence is a grass—often several different varieties of grass. People who love their lawns like to think of them as monocultures but they are actually made up of several different types of either warm-season or cool-season grasses with a number of weeds thrown in to boot.

Appearance

Ancient cultures frequently called anything that ran rather rampantly along the ground "grass." You'll need to do some research to ensure the ingredients you have acquired for the spell you are working on are accurate. A true grass will have a single hollow stem, although clump grasses will have many stems growing together in a bunch. The lower part of each leaf of the plant wraps around the stem to make a sheath. The plant will send up a tasseled flowerhead if allowed to grow for a long enough time—even your lawn grass. If you think you have found a grass and it doesn't fit this basic description, you don't have a grass.

History

What were the old herbalists talking about when they mentioned grass in their spells? Several different types, actually. However, let's talk quickly about what is not a grass. I have already mentioned that clover was called three-fingered grass by some old spellworkers. Five-fingered grass is really *Potentilla erecta*. It is also called cinqeufoil—a great little plant found throughout the United States with plenty of magickal uses, though it's not a true grass. Knotgrass, also known as knotweed, is another great little magickal herb. I rely on it for banishing and hexing. It too is not a grass; it is *Polygonum maculosa*, syn. *P. persicaria*, or possibly *P. aviculare*.

When the old witches and mages did get their hands on what we would call a grass, they had several go-to plants. One of the most common ones was witchgrass. Even here, confusion exists. There are at least four terms that are used interchangeably in the magickal world—witchgrass, couch grass, quack grass, and dog grass. We are either talking about *Elymus repens* (syn. *Agropyron repens*) or *Panicum capillare*. I have seen every one of these common names tied to every one of these scientific names.

Which is which? Will you have a problem if you need *A. repens* and you actually harvest *E. repens*? A few of the folks who visit my friend's shop think so. She likes to relate a story about carrying witchgrass in her shop. When people came asking for dog grass, she would point them to witchgrass and tell them it was basically the same thing. That worked for the majority of people. Others were adament they had to have dog grass. No amount of assurance would sway them, and they would typically leave in a huff. Eventually, she started packaging up the material seperately both as witchgrass and dog grass—same price, same recommendations on use. If anyone asks, she points out that it's the same plant.

I'm pretty much a stickler for getting the right plant for the right purpose. That said, you shouldn't get hung up on common names. As I have said over and over again, find the proper Latin name for the plant you want, and research the many names it might have been assigned by different cultures or in different periods of history. Beyond that, don't lose any sleep over it. In my opinion, all these wild grasses are used for the same purposes.

Uses

Most often, these grasses are assigned to Jupiter, sometimes Mars, and sometimes Mercury. They protect, hex, bind, and promote lust. They are used to stuff poppets. When you get to the information on juniper, I explain how to create an aspering wand and ritual broom. Use the same directions to create these tools with wild grasses if you like. Southern root workers braid long blades of these grasses to use to smudge ritual space. You are advised to braid the grass tightly while it is green and let it dry before using it.

As you scout your neighborhood for wild grass, take a close look at it. Where wild grass grows, it puts down tenacious roots. It lays claim to its turf, so to speak, and doesn't let go. One of the reasons farmers so despise witchgrass is that it will commandeer a field and grab all the water and nutrient resources for itself.

Take a moment to feel the edges of the wild grass blade you pick. Some have a smooth edge but many have a sawtooth edge. Anyone who has had to wade through an abandoned field knows what it is like to come out on the other side with little razor cuts on unprotected legs from those sawtooth edges. If you come across a stand of pampas grass (*Cortaderia selloana*), you can experience this reality firsthand.

As a landscaper, I used to hate pulling up to a prospective client's home and seeing a stand of pampas grass in late winter. I knew the homeowner was looking to dump his or her grass pruning off on me. Working with or around the plant is a nightmare, despite the beauty of a healthy stand of pampas. The blades of pampas grass are like serrated kitchen knives. Any plant with this kind of defense will be great for defensive and protective magick.

This problem doesn't exist with sweet grass. Sweet grass (*Hierochloe odorata*) is as esteemed in many Native American cultures as white sage. Use it to smudge and purify a space or an individual. Ceremonial and decorative baskets are made from sweet grass. Given how hard it is to tell one grass from another, sweet grass does give us a little clue. It smells like vanilla when crushed or burned. If you find sweet grass in your area, the traditional way to use it is to braid the long grass blades into a rope and burn it in the same manner as you would sage.

Finally, remember I said grains are grasses. I like to glean stray plants that invariably come up in the ditches and field edges where grains are planted. (Please don't plunder plants from farmers by gathering plants from their grain stands.) Wheat, rye, barley, rice, corn—these are mostly sacred to fertility goddesses such as Demeter, Ceres, Nidaba, and Corn Mother. You do find some male deities associated with the grain harvest, such as Silvanus, but this area is predominately covered by females.

Overwhelmingly, grains are used for fertility and prosperity. Use them on your altar at Lughnasadh and Mabon or any time to honor the harvest.

CRAFTING: Banishing Whip and Spell

If you want to get rid of a problem, try whipping it with a grass braid. On a Wednesday or Thursday during a waning moon, gather a large bundle of the long grass blades you see growing on the side of a road or the edge of a field. You can also use the razor-bladed leaves of pampas or *Miscanthus* grass that grows as an ornamental in some landscapes.

While the material is still fresh, braid it into a short rope. The easiest way to do this is by tying the grass into one bunch with yarn or twine. Then, separate it into three bunches and braid like you might a ponytail. If you don't have a helper to hold the tied end, clamp it to a table with an alligator clip. When it is braided, tie that end firmly so that the braid doesn't come undone.

At night during a waning moon, set up your altar with a black candle. The incense you use can be copal or dragon's blood or sage. Bring a representation of your problem into your ritual area. This could be the problem described on a piece of page. It could be a poppet that represents the problem. Don't make a poppet of a person for this spell, as you will be stirring up some fairly mean energy. You want to banish the problem, not the person (assuming you believe a person is the source of your problem).

After calling your patron deities for protection, light the candle and incense. Stare intensely at the paper or poppet. See it as the source of your problem. Let your frustration come to the surface as you walk around and around the problem, going widdershins. Use your grass whip to lash out at the problem. Yell at it, if that feels right. Tell it you want it gone. Banish it by slapping it repeatedly with your grass whip. Continue until you are spent or until you feel you have made your point.

Now, burn the poppet or paper along with the whip. If you can't burn these materials, bind them together. Once you have thanked your protectors and opened your circle, take the material and bury it. If you can't bury it, dispose of it in a dumpster well away from your home.

As with anytime you do banishing work, shower afterward to wash away any negativity. Mentally close the door on the problem and remind yourself not to open the door to it again. If you can't wash, smudge yourself thoroughly with incense. Have a soothing cup of chamomile or lavender tea to help calm yourself and be at peace with what you have done.

HOLLY

Latin Name: *Ilex*

Locations: Landscapes, forests

Parts Used: Leaves, berries, wood

Hardiness Zones: 5 to 11

Planetary Ruler: Mars

Uses: Protection, marriage, luck, dream magick; the wood is used for tools.

Edibility: The leaves of hollies are nontoxic.

Warning: Holly berries are poisonous.

Hollies are so popular in the landscape that it's no wonder there are many imposters out there. So before I begin with holly, let's eliminate the look-alikes. The imposters in this case are most often mahonia and certain species of *Osmanthus*. You tend to find leatherleaf mahonia (*Mahonia bealei*) in most landscapes. A quick look at the spiny leaves will tell you this isn't an *Ilex*. The leaves grow opposite one another along the stem. Another tell is the lovely spikes of yellow mahonia flowers that appear in late winter, followed by dusty blue berries in summer. Hollies have inconspicuous white flowers. They produce black or red berries, depending on the varieties.

Use the same leaf trick to identify *Osmanthus fragrans*. Osmanthus leaves grow opposite each other, unlike the holly leaves that grow alternately.

Appearance

Generally, people think of the spiny holly of Christmas when they think of holly. But Japanese small-leaf hollies (*Ilex crenata*) and the broader-leaf Chinese hollies (*I. cornuta*) in the landscape work just as well. Japanese hollies are frequently mistaken for boxwoods. The easiest way to tell them apart from boxwood is to look at the leaves. Boxwood leaves have a smooth edge, while the leaves of the holly, even the small ones, have a bit of a scallop to the edge. You will also see boxwood leaves appearing opposite of one another along the stem. If there is a leaf on one side of the stem, there is another leaf directly across from it (assuming there is no insect or animal damage).

Holly leaves cross alternately along the stem. There is one leaf on the stem, then on the other side the next leaf appears a fraction of an inch further up the stem. And so it goes, all along the branch.

Finally, holly leaves are stiffer than boxwood leaves, whether you are talking about the big spiny leaves of the American holly (*I. opaca*) or the spineless leaves of the inkberry holly (*I. glabra*).

Size isn't a good determining factor when trying to indentify holly. Hollies can range in height from 18 inches to 40 feet tall, depending on the species. They can be low and mounding in form, naturally rounded, columnar, or pyramidal in shape. This plant family truly has a lot of diversity.

Uses

Primarily, hollies are protective plants. As Mars herbs, the leaves are used for protection and to ward away evil spirits. That's why they became popular landscape shrubs. It seems even today, people see the practical advantage of using spiny hollies for protection. In 2012, in an interview with British police, the London-based newspaper the *Telegraph* recommended the use of holly along with 29 other landscape plants as a means to deter burglars.[41] Some things never change.

Holly isn't just for protection. Our Roman, Celtic, and Nordic ancestors brought the plant indoors in the depth of winter to remind themselves that there is life after the dark times ended. It brings good luck to the home during Yule. Holly is considered to be good for marriage spells, especially when paired with ivy, and useful in dream magick.

The leaves aren't the only parts considered protective. Pliny the Elder quoted Pythagoras as saying, "a staff made of the wood,

---

41. "The 30 Plants That Can Help Protect Your Home Against Burglary," *Telegraph*, February 27, 2012, https://www.telegraph.co.uk/news/newstopics /howaboutthat/9108641/The-30-plants-that-can-help-protect-your-home -against-burglary.html.

if, when thrown at any animal, from want of strength in the party throwing it, it falls short of the mark, will roll back again towards the thrower, of its own accord—so remarkable are the properties of this tree."[42] In other words, even if you're a lousy shot, if you fling a holly staff at a charging beast of the wild woods and miss, the staff will come back to you like a boomerang. I would not try to put this to test in the real world, if I were you.

We'll have to take Pliny's word for this. Pythagoras left no physical records. However, his contemporaries and those who followed him must have had some form of documents with his teachings because they quote and reference him extensively.

Not many of us feel the need to have a holly staff, but you can still use the leaves. Gather them in an increasing moon, preferably in the sign of Mars. Use them in any protective incense to enhance the energy of that spell.

CRAFTING: Banishing Spell 1

I don't encourage the use of baneful spells. That said, you may sometimes find that you need to "needle" someone to push them out of your life. In this case for a baneful purpose, use the waning or dark moon as a time to gather the leaf of a spiny holly to write the name of the offending person on. Lightly wipe the leaf with oil or spread it with an aerosol cooking spray, then sprinkle it with red pepper. Set up your altar and create protections around your ritual space. Burn frankincense or dragon's blood incense.

Using a red or black candle as your focus, pass the leaf through the flame as you imagine that person packing

---

42. Pliny the Elder, *Natural History,* bk. 24, ch. 72.

up and moving away. You don't have to wish harm on the person. You just want them out of your life. That can mean a move to a different city, or it can mean something comes along that takes that person's attention away from you. When you can no longer focus on that intent, carefully burn the leaf and flush the ashes down the toilet.

HONEYSUCKLE

Latin Name: Lonicera

Locations: Landscapes, roadsides

Parts Used: Flower, vine

Hardiness Zones: 4 to 9

Planetary Ruler: Mercury, Venus, Jupiter

Uses: Money, good luck, to keep secrets, memory, and psychic powers

Edibility: Sipping the nectar from the flowers is safe.

Warning: The leaves, stems, and other plant parts are mildly toxic.

When North Americans talk about honeysuckle today, they are usually refering to the Japanese honeysuckle (*L. japonica*), a non-native, evergreen vine that is either a delight or a scourge depending on your point of view. If you are trying to reclaim a plot of land overrun with the vine, it is a royal pain in the derriere. If you are lounging on the patio in the evening in late spring and catch a whiff of its fragrant flowers, it is a true delight.

Appearance

Honeysuckle grows as both a vine and a shrub. The vine is an aggressive climber with oval, deep green leaves that are evergreen except in the coldest climates in the United States. *L. japonica* was introduced to the United States around 1806, escaped to the woods, and has been a pervasive presence ever since. It flowers very fragrantly in late spring, bearing flowers in pairs, first white and then maturing into a buttery yellow in the roughly forty-eight hours that the flowers survive on the plant. These are followed by black berries, which area wildlife love. This explains one of the reasons for the vine's pervasiveness.

Our native vining honeysuckle, *L. sempervirens,* or trumpet honeysuckle, is another semi-evergreen vine that is less invasive but also less fragrant. The leaves are oval, a lighter green than the Japanese variety, and larger as well. There are plenty of bush honeysuckles out there too. If you are fortunate enough to have a winter honeysuckle (*L. fragrantissima*), you have a wonderful reminder in the depth of winter that there is hope of spring. Winter honeysuckle is a sweet-smelling tall shrub that perfumes the air in January and February, especially around older homes. It has the same olive-green oval leaves as its vining cousin and a smaller flower that blooms in white.

It should be noted that almost all varieties of honeysuckle are considered to be invasive in the United States, including the lovely *L. fragrantissima.*

History

Remember when I said in chapter 1 that plant identification can pose some questions in magick? In this case, I'm not talking about misidentification. I'm talking about looking at an old grimiore, seeing a spell that calls for a specific plant identified by its common name, and assuming this will be the same plant you can find in our backyard.

Honeysuckle is a good example of this kind of glitch in our magickal system. Maud Grieve tells us when you read about the uses for honeysuckle in the books written by old herbalists like Culpeper, the authors are talking about *L. caprifolium* or *L. periclymenum*, vining plants that would have been found in Europe and the Middle East.[43]

The vine is tough and fibrous. Braiding several lengths together can provide a quick temporary lashing. It's value as an animal fodder is mainly for goats. It is valued for its medicinal uses as an anti-inflamatory and a respiratory aid and its ability to help relieve digestive disorders. Because parts of the plant are mildly toxic, it should only be used under the care of a skilled naturopath.

Uses

I must apologize for the multiple listings for the planetary ruler for this plant. The authorities are in some disagreement here. Nicholas Culpeper attributes it to Mercury, possibly due to its medicinal use at the time for respiratory ailments. Scott Cunningham assigns it to Jupiter. Honestly, I've seen it attributed in

---

43. Maud Grieve, *A Modern Herbal,* vol. 1 (New York: Harcourt, Brace & Co., 1931; Reprint, Dover Publications, 1971), 410.

other sources to Venus and the moon. I'm afraid ancient sources fail us this time around.

What I can tell you is that the flowers are said to be used to attract money or rubbed on the forehead to increase psychic powers. The fragrance of the flowers or incense is said to "sweeten" the energy of a spell or, when used as an anointment, cause those we encounter to like us. This may be where honeysuckle gets its association with fairies and glamoury magick.

You can derive one type of use from the very nature of the plant—that of binding. Several of the old sources say honeysuckle is a good luck herb for marriage and romantic engagements. An anonymous poet in the 1500s in England wrote the following:

> And tho(se) that weare chaplets on their hede
> Of fresh Woodbine (honeysuckle), be such as never were
> To love untrue in word, thought, ne (and?) dede (deed),
> But aye steadfaste …[44]

The herb can be included in wedding bouquets and used as an essential oil in candles for use by consenting couples. The flowers of honeysuckle are not toxic and can be used to flavor communal beverages.

It may occur to some readers that honeysuckle can be used in binding spells of a less than benign purpose. Please keep in mind that binding someone against their will in a romantic way is never recommended. The karmic results, from what I have seen, are nasty for the spellworker and for the victim.

---

44. Henry N. Ellacombe, *The Plant-Lore & Garden-Craft of Shakespeare* (London: Edward Arnold, 1896; Reprint, Dover Publications, 2017), 133 (parentheses mine).

CRAFTING: Prosperity Wreath

You can use this herb to "bind" good fortune and prosperity to you. Making an attractive good luck wreath for your home or altar is an excellent use of this resource. This work should be done in an increasing moon. If it is possible to do so on a Thursday or in the hour of Jupiter, so much the better.

Honeysuckle vine is a very forgiving material to work with, if you find fresh vine. It is much gentler to work with than grape vine, in my experience. You can make the wreath as large as your inspiration or available material allows, but it might be best to start small.

Gather 1 long piece of vine, roughly 15 feet in length. The vine should be fresh and about as thick as a forefinger but not less than a pencil's girth. Beginning at the large end of the vine, make a circle about 8 to 10 inches across. Continue looping the vine for 3 more circles, just like coiling up a garden hose.

Holding the 5 loops in one hand, begin weaving the rest of the vine around and around the loops like a ribbon around a Maypole. To do this, you reach into the center of the loops you have created and pull all of the remaining vine through. In this case, you are working to the right, or deosil. Don't try to force the vine, but make it as snug as possible. You should find that each wrap is about 3 to 4 inches apart.

As you continue around the wreath, the wraps will naturally end up next to each other. Continue wrapping the vine around and around the circle. The end of the vine can be "threaded" back into the body of the circle.

Dress your prosperity wreath with pyrite "glitter" (ground pyrite), dried acorns and other nuts, dried orange peels, and moss. Dab it with patchouli oil or, if you prefer, clove oil. The pyrite glitter can be attached by putting spots of glue on the vine and sprinkling the mineral on it before the glue dries. Use the same method to attach some coins to the wreath as well if you like.

Finish your wreath by wrapping a bright green ribbon around it or by attaching an appropriately sized green bow. Your talisman is now ready to be placed on your altar. Make a large one to hang on the door of your home. Either one can serve as a visual reminder to yourself and the universe to bring prosperity into your life.

IVY

Latin Name: Hedera

Locations: Landscapes, flower baskets

Parts Used: Leaf, vine

Hardiness Zones: 4 to 9

Planetary Ruler: Saturn

Uses: Protection, healing, and dispelling negativity

Edibility: Inedible

Warning: All plant parts are toxic when eaten, especially the foliage. The sap may cause contact dermatitis.

Ivy, or *Hedera,* comes and goes in esteem in the landscape. At one time, people admired "Ivy League" schools as bastions of sage wisdom. Images of ivy-covered castles carry us away in wild fantasies. Today, all many people see when they look at ivy-festooned buildings is an invasive vine that is pulling the mortar right out from between the bricks.

To be clear here, I am talking about ivy, the evergreen vining plant, not poison ivy (*Toxicodendron radicans*), the toxic weed that causes contact dermatitis in varying degrees of severity. Poison ivy is that deciduous wild plant your mother warned you about: "Leaflets three. Let it be."

You may also stumble across a perennial plant called ground ivy (*Glechoma hederacea*). It is a low-growing weed with kidney-shaped leaves. The dead giveaway to ensure you don't mistake this for either poison ivy or true ivy is the pungent odor that comes from the leaves when crushed. I understand beer makers, like their ancient Saxon forerunners, make an ale flavored with ground ivy as a substitute for hops. The smell is a bit too acrid for me, but then I don't like overly hoppy beers either.

Appearance

But I am getting away from our main topic, which is ivy. *Hedera* has leaves that are palmate when young, which is just another way of saying the leaf has five points. It might remind you of a maple leaf. On some fancy varieties of ivy, the points can be very pronounced, and you may see these sold as needle-leaf ivies. Most ivies are some shade of medium to dark green, but you can also find yellow and white variegated varieties. You know you have found a mature vine when you see leaves that are heart shaped.

The change in shape from leaves on young ivy vines and those on older portions of the vine has to do with something called the "cone of juvenility." Interesting to know but beyond the scope of this book. Just be aware that if you find a vine with both types of leaves, you haven't discovered a new mutant form of ivy. It's a natural feature of a mature ivy plant. A mature ivy vine makes flowers and berries late in the season. The berries are toxic, so please avoid collecting or using them.

History

Ivy is not native to the United States. It was brought over by Europeans to remind them of home. Ivy was often hung above the doors of alehouses to signal the availability of the draft.

Ivy is associated with Saturn. Ivy was special to other deities too. The Greeks attributed the vine to Dionysus in part, we're told, because ivy grew abundantly on the island where the god of wine was born. Dionysus and Bacchus are frequently depicted with wreaths of ivy on their heads. Some sources say you can prevent intoxication by either drinking an infusion of ivy or carrying the plant on your person, but don't drink a tea of ivy—it is mildly toxic. I rather doubt carrying ivy will do you much better than carrying amethyst when it comes to drinking. At best, it would be a tangible reminder not to over-imbibe. A better strategy is not to over-imbibe.

Some legends claim Dionysus used ivy to bind a fatal wound on the Greek deity of love Hymenaeus. In Celtic legend, when the lovers Tristan and Isolde die, the king tries to keep them apart through eternity by burying them in separate plots. But a sprig of ivy grew from each lover's grave. Eventually the sprigs found each other and twined together. Every time the king had the vines cut down, the ivies grew back, proving the enduring triumph of true love. If you have ever wondered why sprigs of ivy feature in so many wedding bouquets, now you know.

There are also the familiar legends used in Christian themes that make holly masculine and ivy feminine perhaps because of its clinging, binding nature. In old Pagan traditions, ivy was and still is generally considered to have feminine energy just as holly is said to have masculine energy. In medieval carols, the holly tends to master the ivy. I suspect the church leaders of the time used the imagery to reinforce a preference for male dominance over that of females while at the same time encouraging their flock to think of this most Pagan plant as somewhat inferior. That could be my modern #MeToo bias showing.

Uses

Ivy protects and heals, as you can see in the legend of Dionysus and Hymenaeus. Ivy growing on a house protects. If it falls off and dies, misfortune is on the way. Its evergreen nature conveys the spirit of an energy that goes on and on. That may be why traditions arose that say to give a friend an ivy leaf was to ensure a long friendship. Once, long ago, I read an author who insisted that a dried ivy leaf was virtually a must-have as a bookmarker for a Book of Shadows.

I have found no reliable sources that give credence for the idea of using ivy to ensure a long friendship. However, given that ivy is used to bind, I see no reason to disbelieve it could be used to keep consenting adults together.

CRAFTING: Friendship Spell

If you want to "preserve" a friendship, you can give your friend a talisman of a bookmarker made of a dried ivy leaf.

Select an attractive small leaf in a waxing moon. I used to tell people to put leaves between the pages of an old phone book to dry them. The old phone directories were usually large, heavy, and made of porous paper. They were great drying tools. These days, I doubt anyone under the age of thirty has ever seen a phone book.

No matter. You can place your leaf flat between 2 paper towels and slip this between some heavy books. After a couple of days, remove the leaf and place it between 2 pieces of wax paper. Using an iron and a sturdy level surface, run the iron over the wax paper until the leaf is safely encased. Once the paper has cooled, you can carefully cut away the excess, leaving only the leaf with a roughly ⅛-inch edge of wax paper.

This can be glued to a piece of card stock of white, yellow, pink, or blue. For added effect, thread a couple of rose quartz beads on yarn and make a short tassle to attach to the card stock. Before giving to your friend, hold the talisman and meditate on all the qualities you like and admire about him or her. Fill it with positive (but not possessive) energy. Give it to your friend with the wish that you continue to enjoy each other's good company.

JUNIPER

Latin Name: *Juniperus*

Locations: Landscapes

Parts Used: Leaf, berries, wood

Hardiness Zones: 3 to 9

Planetary Ruler: Sun

Uses: Healing, cleansing, exorcism, and love

Edibility: Depends on the variety

Warning: Common juniper (*Juniperus communis*) is safe for human consumption. However, certain types of landscape junipers—e.g., *J. sabina* and *J. oxycedrus*—are not.

Juniper is an herb of the sun. So many different varieties can be found, from the low-growing Blue Pacific juniper (*J. conferta* 'Blue Pacific') to the knee-high Sargents juniper (*J. chinensis* var.

sargentii) to tree form columns of prickly *J. communis*. Even the tree commonly known as the Virginia red cedar is actually a juniper (*J. virginiana*). The plant is so widespread you can find it on every continent except Antartica, from the highest mountains to the lowest valley.

Appearance

Juniper offers a variety of colors. Generally, it will be a basic green, but it can also be variegated yellow, soft blue, lime green, and, in some junipers during cold weather, burgundy or purple. Junipers make berries but do so very slowly. The plants have to be mature. You may have to look very closely to find the berries on some varieties. Don't be afraid to lift the branches of low-growing groundcover junipers on your search. Junipers produce either scalelike leaves similar to a cypress or leaves with needlelike points.

History

This second type of leaf is why many junipers have fallen out of favor in the landscape. I have always loved all of the members of the juniper family. In the first home I owned as a young adult, I was happily explaining to a friend my plans to landscape the front yard with a variety of junipers. I could tell he was not very impressed. When I asked him why, he replied, "I don't know. I just don't like those sticky plants. I feel like I can walk up and hug a maple tree. I don't think I would want to hug a juniper."

Needless to say, his lack of enthusiasm didn't stop me from going ahead with my plans. But his view is reflected in the landscapes I see around many homes. Fewer junipers grace foundations and natural areas. Instead you see some of the junipers' softer cousins like cypress (*Cupressus*) and arborvitae (*Thuja*).

Beyond landscape uses, juniper is typically considered a timber resource. Of those species that are edible, the berries are used to make gin, brandy, beer, and a sauce for gamebirds. Of course, the essential oil has plenty of medicinal uses.

Uses

All of these are wonderful plants in the landscape and easy enough for the witch to find without much trouble. But you don't want to conflate them in your magick. First, junipers are governed by Jupiter, cypress by Saturn. These two deities would not play well together. Juniper is for healing, and cypress is for comfort, especially at death. Think of cypress as another one of those psychopomp herbs. Juniper is all about the day; cypress is an herb I would associate more with night.

Juniper berries are great for cleansing, either the person or the home. Burning an incense with the berries is calming and exorcising. The size of the berries will vary depending on the type of juniper you find around your area. Virginia cedar berries are dusty blue and about the size of BB pellets. Torulosa junipers (*J. chinensis* 'Torulosa') are tree-form junipers that have blue berries about the size of mature green peas.

CRAFTING: Asperging Wand

The foliage of junipers is healing and uplifting. Gather it to guard against accidents and illness. The foliage is excellent for the construction of a temporary asperging wand or besom.

You asperge with water to cleanse and purify a ritual space or an individual. You can also asperge a room or home to cleanse it of negative energy. Of course, you can simply use your hand to sprinkle droplets of water around an area but the asperging wand is much more efficient.

To make an asperging wand, you will need a stick about 12 inches long and about as big around as your fore-finger. This can be a piece of juniper wood. You will also need some juniper stems with roughly 6 inches of foliage. Four to 6 should make a reasonably full asperger.

This size tool can be constructed using a heavy yarn or garden twine. Simply start by securely tying one of the stems to the bottom of the stick about 3 inches up from the base. Once it is firmly attached, add another stem to the left of the first and tightly wrap the twine around both stems. Continue adding stems, firmly wrapping each one as you go, until the tool is as full as you would like.

Tie the yarn in a double knot. To make the asperging wand a bit more decorative, you can continue wrapping the yarn or twine around until you have a 2-to-3 inch collar around the top of the stems. Tie the yarn off and tuck the knot under the last 2 circles of yarn.

This is a quick, temporary tool that will serve you well for several rituals or workings. You can make it as fancy as you like by wrapping the handle in colored ribbons that coordinate with the seasons or the purpose of your working.

CRAFTING: Besom

Once you've mastered the technique of wrapping an asperging wand, it's just a matter of thinking bigger to make a besom. A besom is a broom made of twigs. You are probably accustomed to seeing brooms made of straw.

Technically, this is a type of sorghum (*Sorghum bicolor*), specifically the tassled tops of the sorghum.

Up until the 1800s, people commonly made their own brooms out of any twiggy material they had at hand. These brooms were pretty much what I will be describing—a long sturdy stick with some type of material tied to the end using a strong hemp or woven rope. The flat, spread-out head of the straw broom wasn't invented until around the 1830s. Because this type of broom did a better job of gathering up dirt and debris, it quickly left the old handmade versions in the dustbin.

But, since you will be using your besom for ritual purposes, the old ways still work just fine. Find a stick roughly 4 to 6 feet long and at least 1 inch in diameter. This will be your handle. In this case, cutting a piece of juniper for the handle is probably not going to be practical, especially if all you can find around your area are shrub-form junipers. Since the top of our besom will be juniper, a sun herb, it would be nice to find a stick from a willow or maple tree to balance our masculine energy with some feminine energy, but use what you can find.

Because this will be a heavier tool, you will need something stronger than yarn to tie the juniper stems to the handle. Leather strapping would be ideal. You can use a very sturdy garden twine as well. In a pinch, clothesline rope will also work.

The stems you cut for the head of your besom should be 12 to 18 inches in length. Follow the instructions given for the asperging wand for tying the stems to the handle. In this case, I recommend tying one circle of stems to the bottom 6 inches of the handle. Then, move up another 6 inches and tie another circle of stems to the handle. This will make for a nice, full besom. Just like the asperging wand, you can finish the tool by creating a collar on the upper 6 inches, wrapping the entire top of the stems with your leather strapping or twine to give the tool a finished look.

This should serve you well for multipe rituals throughout the Wheel of the Year.

MIMOSA

Latin Name: *Albizia julibrissin*

Locations: Fields, roadsides

Parts Used: Flower, leaf

Hardiness Zones: 6 to 9

Planetary Ruler: Saturn

Uses: Protection, purification, prophetic dreams, love, and breaking hexes

Edibility: Edible

Warning: None

Mimosa is a traditional Southern tree. At least it has been since the 1700s. The tree was introduced into the United States from China as an ornamental around 1785 by a botanist who lived in Charleston, South Carolina. It escaped the confines of that lovely city and the rest is Southern history.

This is one of the few plants described in this book that probably isn't seen in Northern states. Mimosa is cold hardy to zone 6a. That takes the plant as far north as the line between Maryland and Pennsylvania, west to southern Illnois and Missouri, around the southern end of the Rocky Mountains, and up the western coastline.

Appearance

This is a fast-growing tree that typically gets about 20 feet tall with an equal spread. You see it most often on the edge of fields and in waste areas. The leaves are tiny, held along a stem in such as way as to look a lot like a mature fern frond. The broad, ferny canopy is what draws a lot of people to the plant.

Gorgeous frilly pink and white flowers are another attraction to the plant. People aren't the only ones fascinated by mimosas in bloom. Bees, hummingbirds, and butterflies like them too.

The tree is deciduous, and this is where the fascination with mimosas fades for humans. The leaves are fine textured and hard to rake. The flowers come on in June, last into July, and then fall off, making a sticky mess on drives and patios. What follows is long seed casings that look like giant bean pods. Because mimosas are very resilent trees, quite a lot of those seeds can sprout. The US Department of Agriculture considers it to be an invasive weed.

History

If you recall, at the beginning of this chapter I told you that sometimes a plant has a close association with a magickal plant and will occasionally adopt the same correspondences. Mimosa falls into this category.

When Scott Cunningham writes about mimosa, he is talking about *Acacia dealbata*.[45] *A. dealbata* is commonly known as the yellow mimosa and sometimes silver wattle. It is commonly known as silk tree or occassionally Persian silk tree, names that are also applied to *A. julibrissan*.

If all this wasn't confusing enough, you can also find a perennial plant growing along the roadside and in deserted areas in the South that has the proper name, *Mimosa pudica*. It looks a lot like a tiny *A. julibrissan* tree. It has the interesting habit of folding up when touched, which is what gives the plant its common name of sensitive plant. This trait has caused the sensitive plant to be used in spells in some African traditions in the South to induce shame into a person.

When I worked as a gardener for a retirement home, I used a specimen of sensitive plant in my horti-therapy demonstrations for those residents who couldn't get outside. Unfortunately, some of the elderly residents kept poking at it and finally worried the plant to death. The folding action is a defense mechanism. Let's face it—whether you are a plant or a person, if you stay constantly on the defensive, it can wear you out.

If you trace all these plants—*Albizia, Acacia,* and *Mimosa*—back far enough, you will find they are all in the Fabaceae family of plants. Given that and the fact that our Southern mimosa tree has been commonly accepted and used in the same manner as the acacia trees of old, I have no problem continuing the tradition.

---

45. Cunningham, *Cunningham's Encyclopedia of Magical Herbs*, 173.

Uses

Mimosa can be used in incense to break hexes. This is definitely an aspect of the yellow mimosa plant. The bright yellow blossoms of the A. *dealbata* tree were seen by the herbalists of old as miniature suns. Their bright coloring and solar energy could burn away negativity and keep it at bay. You can use the solar-sensitive leaves of the mimosa tree in your protection incenses to guard your home or person from the same types of negativity.

A tree of Saturn, the mimosa leaves and flowers promote prophetic dreams, especially when used in a warm bath. Because you will be trying to achieve something of an altered state of consciousness, you should really do this ritual while sober. Alcohol and substances that affect your mind would not make a good combination with a deep meditative ritual. You won't be able to tell the difference between a drug-induced flight of fancy and a true revelation. Plus, you don't want to take a chance of drowning!

Combine the leaves and flowers with rose petals and cornflower blossoms. Add them to the bathwater. If possible, take your bath in candlelight. Burn sandlewood and or rose incense. As you relax, breathe deeply, letting your mind wander freely. What you want to achieve is a state of lucid dreaming in which you are not quite asleep and still not awake. You are in the twilight between worlds.

You can prepare yourself by meditating on a specific question before you step into the bath. Or you can ask your patron deity to speak to you with information that you might need in your life.

Don't be disappointed if you don't achieve a lucid dreaming state at first. It may take several tries. In this case, patience is a virtue. It helps to have paper and pen nearby for when you come out of your dream state. Images that seem so vivid at first can quickly fade. Other images that don't seem to make sense can reveal a purpose when you review your notes at a later time.

CRAFTING: Dream Pillow

If the idea of a dream bath doesn't appeal to you, you may find that creating a dream pillow will work. Sew together two 12-by-18-inch rectangles of good cotton or silk on 3 sides. Add enough batting to make a pillow 2 to 3 inches thick. Before sewing up the fourth side, add 1 cup each of dried mugwort leaves, mimosa leaves (you can include mimosa flowers to make 1 cup total, if desired), and lavender blossoms.

On nights during which you would like to try prophetic dreaming, prepare yourself as you would have for the bath by meditating briefly on a particular situation you would like to have answers for. Again, you can simply ask your patron deity to send you any message that you may need in your life at the moment. Keep that notepad and pen handy at the side of the bed. Dream messages have a habit of waking you in the middle of the night. You may believe you will remember the message when the sun comes up. Trust me. You probably won't. Write it down for future consideration while it is fresh in your mind.

MORNING GLORY

Latin Name: Ipomoea

Locations: Fields, gardens, roadsides

Parts Used: Root, seed

Hardiness Zones: 6 to 11

Planetary Ruler: Saturn

Uses: Peace, happiness, and dream magick

Edibility: The leaves and flowers are nontoxic.

Warning: The roots and seeds of *Ipomoea* should not be
  ingested.

Growing up in the foothills of North Carolina, I was one of
those nerdy kids who looked forward to the day when school
would start. I enjoyed most things associated with school, to

be sure—the homework, the book larning, the arts and crafts—frankly, just about everything we did in school.

But one of my most treasured memories involved gazing out the bus window on the long drive to the school building. Given the rural agricultural community I grew up in, we rode by field after field. With the onset of fall, most of the crops had been harvested. What was left were large expanses of stubble, much of it covered in annual morning glories (*Ipomoea* species). In some cases, a field that had been left to rest or "lay fallow" would be throughly overrun with the vine.

Appearance

In among the heart-form leaves tethered to a jumble of vines, trumpet-shaped flowers of pastel blue, pouty pink, shimmering white, and royal maroon carpeted the coarse acres of stubby corn stalk remnants. All morning glory blossoms start their day twisted in a tight spiral, as if by fairy fingers. With first light, they spill open. On special mornings, patches of fog hovered among the flowers like the batting of Grandma's quilts. The scene could make anyone believe in magick.

History

It may come as no surprise then that morning glory is associated with peace and happiness. But you won't know that by searching many of the old grimiores. That's because annual *Ipomoea* species are native to Asia and the Americas. Europe does have a close cousin of *Ipomoea* named *Convolvulus*, often called perennial morning glory. It is from this plant that some rather different correspondences come.

Dioscorides talks of "Elxine Kussampelos," which researchers have interpreted as *Convolvulus arvensis*, the European pest that so confounds farmers. This plant spreads with an aggressive habit. Its soft white flowers do little to win it any support from the folks whose fields it over takes. Dioscorides recommends it as a laxitive.[46] In magick, that is interpreted as a purging herb— something to use to get rid of problems or negativity.

Uses

The growth habit of most morning glories and *Convolvulus* gives us another use—that of binding. Seen in a positive light, binding means protection. The other side of the coin is that of controlling. *Convolvulus* also can be used to create confusion for one's enemies.

The morning glory family of plants has a number of surprises. As you search the fields for either *Convolvulus* or the pastel colored *Ipomoea* species, you will likely come across the small red morning glory, *I. coccinea*. This is another weed that farmers love to curse at and is excellent material for binding magick.

You have probably heard of High John the Conqueror root (*I. purga*). This is a tropical perennial morning glory. It is a protection root without equal in traditions of African, Carribean, southern United States, and Central American people. Actually, it is the tuber that is used. A root serves to anchor a plant and provide the "infrastructure" for the transport of nutrients to the main plant. A tuber is a specialized storage unit that also functions as a means of propagation. Potatoes are tubers, for example. There are stem tubers and root tubers. High John is a stem tuber.

---

46. Dioscorides, *De Materia Medica: Being an Herbal with Many Other Medicinal Materials, Written in Greek in the First Century of the Common Era*, trans. T. A. Osbaldeston and R. P. A. Wood (Johannesburg: Ibidis Press, 2000), 580.

This is getting a bit technical. Here are the important bits you should remember when gathering morning glories for your magick:

First, annual morning glories don't make tubers. You can gather leaves, flowers, and seeds from annual morning glories for use in dream magick and for peace spells. Put them in a gris-gris bag and hang it from the bedpost to protect you from nightmares.

Second, if you live in the continental United States, you are not going to find High John growing along the roadside. It is found in tropical regions. You might find a *Convolvulus* that could have tubers. In that case, you have something you can substitute for High John in a pinch. Good luck digging it up. Bindweed can grow in some pretty miserable conditions—like in a fallow cornfield that has baked into one humongous clay brick under the hot summer sun.

CRAFTING: Growing Moonflowers for Moon Magick

Before I leave this category of plant, I want to mention moonflowers, *I. alba*. Anyone who wishes to honor a moon deity can make a splendid honoring by growing one or more moonflower vines. Even if you aren't interested in planting the vine for a moon god or goddess, you will find this plant lends a special quality to your outdoor esbat, if you can succeed in growing it.

The flowers are vivid white, almost iridescent. They form the traditional trumpet of the morning glory but much larger, up to 6 inches long and 6 to 8 inches across. On a quiet evening, you might actually hear a little "pop" as they unfurl, right around the time the sun goes down.

In addition, unlike annual morning glories, moonflowers are delicately fragrant.

Moonflowers, and for that matter, all morning glories, are grown from seeds. In May, take the seeds from the packet and allow them to soak for a couple of nights in a shallow dish of water. Some gardeners like to scratch the seed with a knife to get the process started. You can also use a nail file to scuff off a bit of the seed coat—just until you see a bit of white showing through.

Plant the seeds in a peat pot in May. The germination rate of moonflowers is low. I recommend putting 2 to 3 seeds per pot. Moonflowers can be slow to sprout, even if you start them indoors where it is warm. Be patient. It can take up to 2 weeks. However, you should see tiny leaves poking up at the end of 2 weeks. Wait until you get several leaves before you take your new plant outdoors. By this time, it will likely be June. Find a sunny spot and set the peat pot in a large container or a flower bed with a trellis for the vine to grow on.

Again, be patient. The first blooms may not show up until August. But when your vine finally blooms, your patience will be rewarded. Moonflowers only last for 1 day. Don't forget to gather the faded blooms for use in future moon magick and protection spells.

MOSS

Latin Name: Bryophyta

Locations: Trees, decaying wood, streams

Parts Used: All

Hardiness Zones: All zones

Planetary Ruler: Sun, Venus

Uses: Luck, money, and Crone magick

Edibility: Edible under supervision

Warning: Mosses are generally unpalatable, dirty, and prone to harboring bacteria in the wild. While technically they can be eaten or used medicinally, such use should only be done under the supervision of a professional herbalist.

Moss is everywhere except perhaps the arid Southwest and saltwater environments. It covers rocks, pads forest floors, and dangles from trees. Without it, it can be hard to imagine a fairy glen or garden.

Appearance

Technically, moss is a type of nonvascular plant. This just means moss doesn't have specific plant tissue for moving water and nutrients throughout its system, unlike all the other plants described in this book. Moss reproduces by spores, not seeds. The structure of moss is very simple and really hasn't changed since before the dinosaurs showed up.

History

Generally, you find moss growing in shaded, damp places. In most cases in the modern world, moss is considered a nuisance, a sign of a problem, not a material to be welcomed. Moss on a foundation wall indicates moisture that might be disintegrating the home's support. Moss on the roof shingles means you might be spending a lot soon to fix a rotting roof. Moss in the lawn could be a sign of several problems, from poor nutrition to soil compaction.

Please note, moss and slime are not the same thing. Moss is a primitive plant. Slime is a primitive fungus. Moss and lichens are not the same thing, although it's not uncommon to hear lichens called moss. For example, oak moss (*Evernia prunastri*) is a lichen that grows on oaks and other hardwoods. However, lichens are also not plants. They are specialized fungi that form a symbiotic relationship with algae to survive.

Irish moss (*Chondrus crispus*) is not moss but a type of algae. While I am at it, Spanish moss (*Tillandsia usneoides*) is not a moss but a member of the bromeliad family. However, Spanish moss tends to get lumped in with mosses in the magickal world and associated with love, healing and—oddly—revenge. Sphagnum moss (*Sphagnum palustre,* syn. *Sphagnum cymbifolium*), you may be relieved to know, is actually a true moss.

Moss is very opportunistic. It grows in cracks in concrete and on bricks. It nestles into rock crevices and swaddles rotting logs. Of all the plants mentioned in this book that someone might take exception to you gathering, moss is one that no one is likely to stop you from picking up. They might look at you like you are crazy for gathering it, but I doubt they would stop you.

Uses

For all the negative associations in today's world, we can still find times when an abundance of moss is pleasing to look at. Tranquil pictures of a moss-covered rock outcropping populate the internet for good reason. Images of bubbling streams don't seem complete without patches of moss dotting the stream banks.

In Asia, especially in Japan, moss lawns are iconic. Granted, the climate in Japan is perfect for growing moss, so if you live there and you don't like moss, you are kind of out of luck. Moss is in the country's national anthem: "May your world go on for thousands of years until pebbles merge into one giant rock and covered with moss."

It has taken several years, but I have finally cultivated a nice covering of moss in and around the labyrinth at the back of my house. I have even given over a portion of my yard to moss. Why not? It beats mowing.

Agrippa assigns moss to the sun and Venus for planetary rulership, although I have seen sources that ascribe it to the moon.[47] Moss is considered good luck, especially in regard to money. This is probably due to its evergreen nature and ability to survive in otherwise stark locations.

Those who follow the Nordic tradition may remember that yellow hair moss (*Polytrichum commune*) is dedicated to Thor's wife, Sif. Sif was known for her beautiful hair until Loki cut it off. His penance was to convince the dwarfs to fashion her a new wig of gold to match the golden locks she lost. Again, you can see an association between moss and prosperity—in this case, gold.

Beyond good luck and prosperity, moss is most often used as a stuffing for poppets. Since moss is known to hold many times its weight in moisture, if you gather it for this purpose, be certain to allow it to thoroughly dry before using it. Otherwise, you may find your poppet will turn into a moldy mess.

CRAFTING: Fairy House

For those interested in attracting the Fae, know that these entities are thought to have a real affinity for moss. In southern Germany and Scandinavian countries, moss folk or wood folk are thought to live among the forest moss. Some are clothed in moss; others spin moss into fabulous fabrics.

You can invite these types of fairy folks into your landscape by creating a place for them to live. Outside, find a shady spot, preferably out of the way of busy foot traffic. Take an old terra-cotta pot and carefully chip a bit of the upper rim of the pot away (if it's not broken out already).

47. Agrippa, *Three Books of Occult Philosophy*, 99.

Check the surrounding area for patches of moss. It's best to get the material from your area because it is already acclimated to your locale. You only need a handful of moss.

In a blender that you're not too attached to, put your moss along with 1 cup of either buttermilk or plain yogurt. Blend until you have a moss slurry.

Outside, dampen your terra cotta pot and brush or pour the slurry all over the pot. You can deposit any extra on the ground around the pot. Keep the area watered until you see the moss start to grow. Then you can back off watering and let nature take its course. Feel free to "decorate" the fairy abode with pretty rocks and crystals, nut hulls, and seed pods from the surrounding area. Your moss fairy home is now ready for occupants.

MUGWORT

Latin Name: Artemisia vulgaris

Locations: Waste areas

Parts Used: Leaf

Hardiness Zones: 3 to 9

Planetary Ruler: Venus

Uses: Scrying teas or incense, astral projection, healing, dream magick, dragon magick, and psychic powers

Edibility: All parts are edible.

Warning: Mugwort (and other artemisias) can be ingested in small quantities but should be avoided in large doses and by women who are pregnant.

Common mugwort, or *Artemisia vulgaris,* is the herb Pagans turn to for psychic awareness. In this book, I am talking mainly about plants that you can find growing naturally around your home from the edge of the road to the depth of the forest. However, artemisias are readily found in many flower beds too.

Appearance

A. vulgaris is governed by Venus. Look for it on roadsides, railway beds, and other waste areas. The leaf is dull green on top but fuzzy silver underneath. Use this tip to tell the difference between mugwort and other weeds because the shape of the mugwort leaf is very similar to other things, like ragweed (*Ambrosia artemisiifolia*).

Cultivated artemisias lend a lovely soft gray look to the flower bed. Most have fine-textured leaves or foliage with gentle hairs that make them feel like velvet. Others, like wild mugwort, are your basic green, sometimes sporting small yellow or unimpressive white flowers late in summer. These are more often grown for medicinal uses. If you have trouble finding wild mugwort, yet have access to it in the landscape, there is no reason why you can't substitute the cultivated type for the wild mugwort.

History

Mugwort has had many practical uses over the years. Its name suggests one use. It derives from the Old English word *mucgwyrt*, meaning "midge or moth plant." The herb was thought to repel moths and other insect pests. It was used to help women with issues relating to menstruation and childbirth—not surprising since this is a Venus herb. It is among the nine herbs sacred to Norse traditions.

Uses

The leaf of mugwort is burned during scrying. Agrippa includes mugwort in the twelve plants of the elemental world, useful for attracting and binding spirits.[48] He advises that smearing mugwort oil on a shiny sheet of steel and then heating it will allow the user to see spirits.[49]

Dried mugwort can be used in a tea to be drunk or as a wash for divination tools. Traditionally, it is said to be good for those trying to achieve astral projection. (Caution: Don't use wild herbs for teas unless you are positive you know what might have been sprayed on them when you're not around.) Speaking of travel, mugwort in the shoes is said to keep the traveler from becoming tired. On the other hand, placing mugwort leaves under the doormat was believed to keep unwanted people from your home.

If you are gathering artemisia from the landscape, there is a possibilty that you will be gathering wormwood (*A. absinthium*), that famous herb used to make absinthe. Assuming your wormwood has not been treated with herbicides or other chemicals, it is safe to use. The stories of wormwood driving people crazy are well overblown.

A teaspoon of dried wormwood in a tea will not have enough thujone, the chemical of concern, to cause you any harm. You would have to consume great qualities of it to have a problem—assuming you could do that in the first place. Artemisias of any sort are very bitter. They were actually used to give beer that "hoppy" taste if hops weren't available. Such use goes all the back to ancient Egypt.

48. Agrippa, *Three Books of Occult Philosophy*, 295.
49. Agrippa, *Three Books of Occult Philosophy*, 134.

As an aside, you may occasionally see spells that call for the combination of mugwort and St. John's wort (*Hypericum perforatum*) that are based on old sources. The translation may be or may not be accurate. Maud Grieve points out in *A Modern Herbal* that in some European countries mugwort was colloquially known as "St. John's plant."[50] Not to say there is any problem with using these two plants together. Actually, since St. John's wort is a masculine sun herb and mugwort is a feminine Venus herb, the two might work well together to balance those energies in ritual.

CRAFTING: Dragon Magick Ritual

Mugwort can also be used in dragon magick. This may be a reference to the Chinese practice of hanging bunches of *A. argyi* around homes and burning the leaves during the annual Dragon Festival. This may also refer to the use of a mugwort tea for dreamwork, an excellent way to reach out to dragons.

If you would like to reach out to dragons, you can try a ritual to ask for their attention. I don't recommend that you try to summon dragons in the way you might summon some spirits or elementals. All you can do is ask them to come to you. They may or may not show up.

I don't think you have to have a particular phase of the moon to do this work. You will need a quiet spot where you won't be interrupted. Brew yourself a cup of mugwort tea using 1 teaspoon of herb to 8 ounces of boiling water. Steep for 5 minutes. You can add rose and sweetner, if you like, to improve the taste.

50. Grieve, *A Modern Herbal*, vol. 2, 556.

Dragons are most often associated with fire and air, but they are also connected to earth and water. Select a candle to match the element you are drawn to. If you can't decide, use black or green. Blend 1 teaspoon each of dragon's blood resin and ground mugwort for your incense.

There is a green and red jasper with epidote and piemontite that is sold as dragon stone. If you can find a piece of this to have in your ritual area, wonderful. If not, proceed without it.

Settle into your space. Light the candle and the incense. Sip on your tea as you quiet your mind. When you are ready, set down the tea and pick up the stone. Open your mind. I wrote this chant to make my request known to any dragons that might be receptive:

Dragon's blood, dragon bone,
Dragon older than the stone.
These humble signs I offer thee
For thy protection over me.

Repeat the chant as often as you need to. Then stop and wait. You may feel the presence of energy; you may not. You may need to repeat the ritual several times. Be patient. If you are sincere in your efforts, you will likely find you will have success. How matters develop from that point forward is up to you.

MULLEIN

Latin Name: *Verbascum thapsus*

Locations: Gardens, fields

Parts Used: Leaf

Hardiness Zones: 3 to 9

Planetary Ruler: Mercury

Uses: Protection, courage, exorcism, and protection against sorcery

Edibility: All parts of mullein are safe for consumption.

Warning: None

Mullein is *Verbascum* and is ruled by Saturn. Its large, oval, fuzzy leaves and tall yellow flower stalk that blooms in early summer make it easy to spot in common areas.

Appearance

Mullein is biennial. That just means the plant needs two years to complete it growth cycle. The first year, the seed sprouts and a rosette of fuzzy, gray, lance-shaped leaves appear. At this point, gardeners might be excused for confusing mullein with another favorite gray plant in the flower bed, lamb's ear (*Stachys byzantina*). As the season goes on, any confusion should fade. For one thing, lamb's ear blooms every year, usually with soft pink or mauve flowers. Mullein won't be blooming in its first year.

Second, if you crush the foliage of a lamb's ear plant, you will notice a distinct apple aroma. Mullein foliage is missing a distinct odor. Finally, when the mullein plant gets ready to bloom, it sends up a long, tall stalk often 4 feet tall or more, topped with a flower spike of 8 to 12 inches. Lamb's ear only wishes it could grow so tall!

History

Mullein is quite a character. In addition to its magickal reputation, it has been put to good use in many other ways. You can tell by the colorful names people have given it over the years. Medicinally, mullein is used for those with respiratory ailments whether from a cold or sore throat. Brewed and strained to remove any fine hairs, the concoction is soothing and mildy sedating. For this purpose, it is called lungwort (not to be confused with *Pulmonaria*).

Given it's soft, downy texture, the name "cowboy's toilet paper" should come as no surprise. In the book *Southern Fields and Forests* by Francis Porcher, published in 1863, the author describes how poor people used mullein leaves as bandages.[51] This seems to be a common thing for both the poor and for soldiers on the battlefields of old. There are plenty of examples of modern survivalist books with recommendations of the medicinal uses of mullein. When used for these activities, the plant is known as feltwort, flannel plant, and velvet plant.

Mullein comes from Europe and Asia, and those folks have been using it for ages. Dioscorides reports a tisane of the yellow blossoms could lighten hair, while the ash from burnt mullein leaves could darken hair.[52] Oddly, mullein didn't get a special name when used for cosmetic purposes.

You will frequently see mullein refered to as candlewick plant or hag's taper. I know of several historical sources that describe how people would cut the soft leaves up into wicks for lamps. Early on in my research into the magickal uses of plants, I came across references to hag's tapers. The idea was that witches used to dip the tops of mullein in fat and carried them as torches on the way to their Sabbats with the Devil. I've seen reference to this practice among ancient Romans at funerals and among miners in the early days of the western expansion in the United States.

Given that the plant, when dried, burns quickly, it's hard for me to imagine how useful tallow-dipped mullein stalks could have been. But I suppose if you're in a hard fix for a light, anything will do. A much more feasible explanation for me is that

---

51. Francis Payre Porcher, *Resources of Southern Fields and Forests, Medical, Economical and Agricultural: Being Also a Medical Botany of the Confederate States, with Practical Information on Useful Properties of the Trees, Plants, and Shrubs* (Richmond, VA: West and Johnson, 1863), 464.

52. Dioscorides, *De Materia Medica*, 655.

the flowering yellow stalk, when viewed from a distance, can look like a tall candle.

Uses

Regardless, wherever it grew in Europe, India, and Asia, mullein developed a reputation as a good plant for protection against bad spirits. Agrippa attributes it to Mercury. This makes sense, given that the plant is associated with respiratory cures. But I have seen sources that say Saturn governs mullein. This may have something to do with its ability to banish negativity and bad spirits.

In today's magickal community, mullein leaf, dried and powdered, is sometimes offered as a substitute for graveyard dust. Some of my associates who practice Hoodoo, Santería, or Voodoo tend to discount its use for this purpose. They insist only the real thing will do. While you're at it, the old rootworkers would have been looking for dirt from the grave of a criminal.

In Western traditions, mullein can be used in incense or gris-gris bags to protect against sorcery, instill courage, and break hexes. Its use for opposing negative energy was so strong, practictioners tell us you only need a mullein leaf slipped into the pillow case to prevent nightmares from haunting your dreams.

CRAFTING: Yarn Guardian

I am sometimes asked what herbs can help children who are bothered by nightmares. I recommend creating a yarn guardian, stuffed with mullein and lavender.

You'll need a skein of yarn in a color that is pleasing to the child. This is a poppet and it can be as big as you like. However, to give the child something to comfortably hold on to through the night, I suggest making the doll at least 8 inches long.

Find some scrap cardboard or a thin book that fits the length you have choosen. The doll can be as full as you like but I would advise wrapping the yarn around and around the form at least 50 times. Gently slip the yarn off the form and tie the loops together with a short piece of yard. For the moment, you have 50 loops of yarn securely tied so that they won't fall apart. Cut the strands at the opposite end. Now you have a yarn mop.

Set it aside for a moment. Take a small square or circle of cloth and add at least 1 tablespoon of chopped, dried mullein and 1 tablespoon of lavendar. This will be the form that fills out the head of the poppet. You can add more herbs if you don't think this is full enough. Gather the edges up and tie this into a secure packet of herbs.

Separate the yarn strands and tuck the herb packet in up close to where you tied the yarn loops together. Gather all the yarn around the packet and tie it with a piece of yarn. This is the head and neck of your doll.

Now divide the yarn below the neck into three bundles. The bundles on either side should have 12 strands and will form the arms of the doll. The rest becomes the body. Carefully braid the yarn on either side and tie the ends off with a piece of string. For the body, you can tie the yarn off in the middle and leave the ends loose for a skirt, or after tying off the middle for the abdomen, you can braid the lower part for legs.

As you work with the poppet, you should be filling it with positive, loving energy for the child. If this is your child, you can periodically spray or dab lavender essential oil on the poppet. If it is for a friend, advise the parent to do this from time to time. Let the child know that this is his or her little guardian spirit who will keep watch over them while they sleep and run away any meanies and monsters that approach.

OAK

Latin Name: Quercus

Locations: Landscapes, forests

Parts Used: Leaf, bark, nut

Hardiness Zones: 3 to 9

Planetary Ruler: Sun

Uses: Protection, fertility, wishes, luck, health, and money

Edibility: All parts are edible.

Warning: None

Oak, or *Quercus,* is well known for lending strength to magick. A sun herb (or some say a Jupiter herb), it has been revered by many traditions in countless countries. In the United States, there are over fifty-eight species of oaks that are native to our country. White oaks (*Q. alba*) and red oaks (*Q. rubra*) are perhaps among the most common, although in the last forty years, landscapers have made willow oaks (*Q. phellos*) a common third-place choice.

Because there are so many varieties of oaks, it's hard to give one set description. The leaves can be simple and lance-shaped, like a willow or live oak, or they can be complex with three or more lobes. To complicate matters a bit more, the lobes can be rounded, like a white oak, or pointed to varying degrees, like a red oak. I can say oaks will likely be one of the tallest trees in the surrounding landscape, and the gray to light brown bark is usually textured with small ridges or fissures.

History

In Eastern coastal communities, live oaks (*Q. virginiana*) are the epitome of aged grace and grandeur. I have always had an awareness of the energy in nature, long before I called myself a witch, but it was on a vacation in South Carolina that I first truly felt that energy. I had stopped at a roadside attraction where a local resident was recounting tales of bygone days to the tourists.

Everywhere you looked, live oaks owned the landscape. They commanded the ground, forbidding any grass to grow. They framed the sky with gnarled branches that seemed to go on forever in all directions, with canopies dense enough to shade the area but not so dense as to blot out the sun.

As I listened, I reached out a hand to brace myself against the ridged bark of one particular tree. I felt a distinct humming energy. Honestly, I thought at first I might be feeling the vibration from nearby road traffic. Then I realized, it was the energy of the tree. The sensation is still mesmerizing for me. I believe that is the power that our ancestors from any culture felt when they learned to venerate the tree.

It doesn't hurt that oak provided them with wood for their homes and fires, food in the form of acorns, tanning material in the form of the tannins in its bark and leaves, and more. Plus, oaks can live for hundreds of years. Think of the grounding effect that must have had in prerecorded history. You see things change around you; loved ones live and die. The one constant would be the stately oaks that sheltered and provided for your family and the family that preceded them and the ancestors who preceded them. It would be easy to imagine that the tribal oak in front of you must live forever.

Uses

Oaks provide many opportunities for use in magick. Any part of the oak offers protection against almost anything. Males can use it for potency by carrying an acorn or a talisman made of oak. Anyone can use it in healing spells such as drawing a bath to which oak chips, an acorn, or some oak leaves are added. The wood makes excellent wands or walking staffs. Finely ground or minced wood can be used in incense for strength or to honor any number of deities to whom it is sacred. The bark is good for this purpose as well.

Across cultures, the wood from an oak that had been touched by lightning was considered especially potent. It was thought, since oaks are sacred to many sky gods, a lightning strike was a sign of the god touching that particular tree. Oaks are often the largest tree in a forest. Lightning will generally seek the most readily accessible target. That oaks are frequently hit is not surprising. The fact that they frequently survive is amazing. Keep in mind that is not always the case. I have an oak in my general vicinity that had its bark blown off by a lightning strike.

Plant an acorn with your wish and the wish is said to come true if the nut sprouts. Carry the wood or bark for good luck. For protection, select a door made of wood for the entries of your home. If you can't afford an oak door, have the door entrance framed in oak. Even the oak moss conveys all the aspects of the mighty oak tree.

CRAFTING: Oak Gall Ink

Oak galls have been used since the time of the Egyptians to give ink staying power. If you read a recipe or spell calling for iron gall, it is the same thing. You will sometimes read that the US Constitution was written in poke ink. It wasn't. Chemical analysis proves it was written with oak gall ink, and you can make it yourself.

To find oak galls in your area, watch for something called flagging on oaks in midsummer. This happens when a particular wasp lays its egg in the tender stem near the end of the oak branch. The gall forms around the damage as the insect inside matures. When the insect emerges, the stem breaks and dangles there like a flag (hence the term *flagging*). In a really bad infestation, the oak tree can look like it was attacked by a weed-whacker.

When the material drops off, you will find what looks like little tan marbles. They will vary in size from ⅛ to ¼ inch in diameter. These can be crushed and boiled in just enough water to cover the material. The result will be black or dark brown in color. The liquid can be added to pokeberry or cherry ink. A pure oak gall ink can be made using copper sulfate, water, and gum arabic to thicken the liquid.

One formula listed in the Greek Magical Papyri is 1 dram of myrrh resin, 4 drams of truffle, 2 drams of blue vitriol (copper sulfate), 2,400 drams of oak gall, and 3 drams of gum arabic.[53] Technically, a dram is a liquid measure and the materials listed above are dry ingredients. But this is a rough formula and you can estimate that one dram is ¾ teaspoon of dry material.

53. Dieter Betz, ed., *The Greek Magical Papyri*, 167.

ONION

Latin Name: Allium

Locations: Everywhere

Parts Used: All parts

Hardiness Zones: 4 to 9

Planetary Ruler: Mars

Uses: Protection, exorcism, and prophecy

Edibility: All parts are edible.

Warning: None

Wild onions (*Allium canadense*) seem to grow everywhere, and they are fairly easy to spot. Just look for the grassy stems of aromatic foliage.

Appearance

What you may assume is wild onion may really be wild garlic (*A. vineale*). It doesn't matter. Both are in the *Allium* genus. Both have basically the same correspondences: protection, banishing, hexing, and, surprisingly, love. Onions have the added characteristic of drawing money.

If you are a stickler for precision, you can tell wild garlic from wild onion by looking at the stems. Wild garlic stems are rounded and hollow. Those of wild onion are flatter and solid. Wild onions are more likely to bunch than wild garlic. In fact, in the lawn and other waste areas, there is no such thing as one wild onion.

Another tell comes when the plant blooms. Yes, as a member of the lily family, all alliums bloom. Garlic gives us a green or purple flower while onion blossoms are generally white or pink.

History

These two plants can be found all over the place and no one, but no one, is likely to complain if you pull them for your own use. Still, you may find some other plants in this family that are considered civilized, especially around old houses. Chives (*A. schoenoprasum*) are cultivated in the herb garden for their milder flavor and attractive blue tops. Leeks (*A. ampeloprasum*) are grown in chef gardens, again because the flavor is less overpowering.

Your grandmother might have grown society garlic (*Tulbaghia violacea*). This is not a true garlic or onion although it is a close cousin. It's great for flavoring salads or dips but not used in magick.

People in the Smokey and Blue Ridge Mountains enjoy a wild allium called ramps (*A. tricoccum*). My father had a good friend who was a truck driving buddy. The two men would occasionally ride together. The only time Daddy declined was in May when his friend would go home to the mountains to collect a good supply of ramps. Ramps are especially fragrant. Daddy said his friend ate so many ramps, he reeked of them. In the days before air conditioning, hauling goods with his friend in the building heat of summer was just impossible, he said.

Uses

Onions are high in sulfuric acid. This is part of what gives them their heat, their smell, and their power of protection in magick. The juice of an onion has many uses, although many of them are unlikely to be embraced in our society. Since knives and swords were once drawn over a cut onion to purify them, you can use the same technique to purify ritual tools like athames after use.

You can cut an onion in half and leave it in the kitchen to absorb negativity. A cut onion rubbed in a continuous line all around the entrance to your home will keep enemies away. If onion seems too strong for use in incense, substitute the skins instead. Add the skins to incenses that are blended to increase prosperity.

I'm still not sure how such an odorous plant came to be used for love. It is supposed to promote lust. Another old charm used by young girls was to take two onion bulbs and write or lightly carve the names of potential suitors on them. The onions would be laid by the chimney and watched carefully. The first to sprout would indicate her true mate.

You can eat wild onions and garlic if you are certain they have not been sprayed with pesticides. Cultivated onions (*A. cepa*) might be a safer bet. Onions were thought to protect the family's health, especially over winter, when living quarters are crowded. If you have the space to grow your own onions, you can make a braided onion rope to hang in the kitchen.

Onions are generally grown from bulbs, but you can also find sets in fall and late winter. You can plant them in the spring, but these will typically not mature into full bulbs. Plant onions in full sun in loose, amended soil that drains well. You can also grow onions in a large container if you don't have land on which to plant.

CRAFTING: Braided Ritual Talisman

To have the protective energy of onions readily available at all times, you can make an onion braid to hang in the home. Onions planted in fall should be available to harvest by June or July depending on your location. The signal for when to harvest is that the tops will begin to turn yellow. Lay the yellowing tops over and wait for the tops to turn brown. Carefully dig up the bulbs, clean them, and lay the plants in a warm dry place to dry.

Once that happens, you are ready to braid. This can be an informal spell, or you can set up a circle, calling on Mars or your patron deities to watch over you as you work. Dragon's blood would be an appropriate incense to burn during this activity. The best time to do this work would be on a Tuesday (the day of Mars) and during an increasing moon.

Pick 9 to 12 onions of uniform size. Lay 2 onions on the work area in front of you. Begin the braid by crossing the stems, then lay the third onion plant on top. Bring the foliage of the onion on the right over that of the onion in the middle and lay this foliage between that of the onion on the left and the onion in the middle. Then pick up the foliage on the left, pull it over the foliage from the right, and lay it between the foliage of the middle and right onion.

It may help to think of onions as numbered. The first two onions are 1 and 2. The onion you lay on top is 3. Your initial pattern is 1-3-2. The next move creates 1-2-3. The next move creates 2-1-3. At this point you stop and add a new onion to the middle of the braid. Now you have 2-(1 and 4)-3. Continue the braid. With each new cross, add in another onion until you have used up your supply. Finish by braiding the rest of the foliage all the way to the end. Use red and orange yarn or ribbon to tie your braid off.

This is one of those activities that will make more sense when you actually lay the material in front of you and give it a try. Practice with yarn first to get the knack of it.

Once the braid is completed, pass it through the dragon's blood incense. Focus on the raw energy in the bulbs contributing to keep your home safe. Thank the deities who have helped you. If you have set up a ritual circle, ground yourself and open it. Hang the braid in a warm dry place to cure some more. Once it is thoroughly dry, you can move it into the heart of your home, the kitchen.

This is practical magick. You can and should cut the onions off to use them over time. A good tight braid should hold up on its own; however, it is okay to secure the base with some red yarn. Once all the onions are gone, you can cut up the remaining foliage for use in future incense or use the braid to smudge the home or ritual area as needed.

PERIWINKLE

Latin Name: Vinca minor, V. major

Locations: Landscapes

Parts Used: Flower, leaf

Hardiness Zones: 4 to 9

Planetary Ruler: Venus

Uses: Steadfast love, lust, mental power, funeral rites, protection, and purification

Edibility: It is used medicinally.

Warning: Vinca is mildly toxic.

Periwinkle vine, not the annual flower, is a powerful magickal plant. The summer annual is *Catharanthus roseus*. It has some interesting associations and uses, but that information will be for another time.

Appearance

Called *Vinca minor* or *V. major*, periwinkle is used as a ground-cover in the landscape. The leaves of *V. minor* are dark green, nearly black. The vine is very stringy, forming low-growing mats of foliage. It spreads primarily by rooting at nodes along the stem. In late winter, the sky blue flowers are an early indicator that spring is coming.

V. major is more aggressive and rambunctious. The leaves are larger, more rounded, and a lighter shade of green. While *V. minor* spreads quietly along under bushes and trees, *V. major* rolls over everything in sight. Like *V. minor*, *V. major* has dusty blue flowers, borne a little later in the season than its more well-behaved cousin.

History

In recent years, periwinkle has gained a nasty reputation as a non-native weed. I would have to agree that *V. major* fits that category. I once used a bit of it in a hanging basket thinking, what could be the harm? Toward the end of the season as I changed out my flower displays around the yard, I set the basket at the edge of a shrub border and forgot about it. The *V. major* took advantage of my neglience and escaped! That was ten years ago. I am still pulling the stuff out. By comparison, I have had *V. minor* in a planting bed for the entire twenty years I have lived at my current residence. It has never given me any trouble. If it encroaches too much on the azaleas in the bed, I pull some out—no problem.

Uses

If you find periwinkle in the wild, pay close attention. Carl Feagans of the US Forest Service notes that the plant was often used as an ornamental on old gravesites in the 1700s and 1800s.[54] That may not be the case for the patch of periwinkle you find on your nature walk, but I wouldn't discount the possibility entirely.

The association with death is one more aspect of the plant. In Italy, the graves of children who died in infancy were commonly marked with the plant. This tender use illustrated the plant's reputation as an herb of remembrance, not of morbid loss.

I mentioned in chapter 3 that the old grimoires recommended addressing the plant as "vinca pervinca." That isn't just a poetic turn of phrase. That was the plant's proper name, according to Pliny the Elder, writing in 1 CE, and it means to bind or entwine.[55]

According to Maud Grieve, Apuleius, writing in 1480, gives a very elaborate ritual for gathering the herb. Specifically, the person gathering the plant should be "clean of any uncleanliness." That usually meant the gatherer was not to have indulged in any sexual activity for at least forty days. Periwinkle could be gathered when the moon is nine, eleven, or thirteen nights old—in other words, basically in the waxing moon. The reward for showing such respect was to be "shielded and ever prosperous and undamaged by poisons and by water." Other benefits were protection from the devil or demonic possession, snakes, and wild beasts.[56] To reap these benefits, burn the leaves in an incense to create a zone of protection around yourself or your home.

Since periwinkle is governed by Venus, no one should be surprised that it is used for love. Combine Venus's influence with

54. Carl Feagans, "Wild Plants and Historical Archaeology," *Archeology Review* (blog), April 3, 2018, https://ahotcupofjoe.net/2018/04/wild-plants-and -historic-archaeology/.

55. Pliny the Elder, *Natural* History, bk. 21, ch. 39.

56. Maud Grieve, *A Modern Herbal,* vol. 2, 630.

the evergreen nature of periwinkle and you get everlasting love between spouses. Culpeper recommended the husband and wife should eat the leaves of periwinkle to enhance and maintain their love—please don't do that. Periwinkle was brought to the United States from Europe and the Mediterranean as much for its supposed medicinal value as for its ornamental value. Not much of the reputed medicinal benefits stand up to scrutiny. However, periwinkle consumed in large enough quantities can lower blood pressure. With this in mind, use the leaves and flowers in communal bathes. Dress red candles with the herb for use during your amorous activities. But please, don't eat the periwinkle.

CRAFTING: Letting Go Ritual

This would be a good herb to use at those times when you need to let a loved one go. End of life is a trying time, particularly for the ones left behind. Getting over the sense of loss can seem impossible. A simple ritual involves doing some candle magick in the time of a waning moon. Set up your ritual space according to your tradition. After gathering, drying, and mincing periwinkle, dress a white or blue candle with oil (sandlewood is a good choice) and roll the candle in the dried herb.

Before you begin the ritual, make a tea of juniper, Angostura bitters, and orange zest. Simply steep 1 tablespoon of juniper, 1 teaspoon of orange zest, and several dashes of bitters in boiling water for 10 minutes. If you can use alcohol, you can make this drink with 1 shot of gin, ½ shot of Triple Sec, and a dash or two of bitters. The juniper or gin is for healing, the bitters are for the tears, and the orange or Triple Sec is for the sunshine that comes from healing and happy memories.

With your ritual area set up, feel free to invite any of the chthonic deities to participate. You can also call on your patron deities to aid you. Light the candle and speak with your loved one. Know that he or she can hear you. Tell them what you will miss. Thank them for being a part of your life. If the relationship was strained, forgive them or at least make them a promise to forgive when you have the strength to do so. Cry, scream, or wail if you can.

This used to be called keening in the Celtic community. Importantly, it is an avenue of release. Whether you had a good or bad relationship with the departed, you have to let go. You can't survive the rest of your life tethered to someone who is no longer a part of the mundane world.

When you have exhausted your grief or just can't go on, stop and drink from your wailing cup. Know that you will meet this person again on the other side. It's okay to keep fond memories. You may even need to repeat this ceremony for full closure. That's okay too.

PINE

Latin Name: Pinus

Locations: Landscapes, forests

Parts Used: Leaves, resin

Hardiness Zones: 2 to 9

Planetary Ruler: Saturn

Uses: Healing, cleansing, purifying, strength, and house and business blessing

Edibility: All parts are edible.

Warning: None

I love pines, particularly *Pinus strobus,* or white pine. They were as numerous as oaks in the area where I grew up. White pines were much easier to climb than oaks too. All you had to do was reach the lowest scaffold of limbs and you were set. White pine branches radiate from the trunk in a circle, usually 5 or 6 to a ring. The rings are spaced about 2 feet apart. Once you reached the first circle, you could scamper up the tree as far as you dared and survey the entire world.

My mother was none too pleased. Pines of all sorts ooze a sticky resin at every opportunity. That's great for magickal workings but not so good for clothing. It was not so good for young hands on a school night either. I had quite a few intense scourings at bath time as we tried to scrap that resin off my hands, arms, and face.

Appearance

The white pine's reach extends to Piedmont North Carolina, and the tree is found most often in New England, mid-Atlantic, and Great Lakes states. You can find plenty of other varieties of pines in other parts of the United States, including black pines, yellow pines, scrub pines, Scotch pines, pit pines, sugar pines, loblollies, and the iconic long-leaf pine of the Tar Heel State.

The bark of the white pine is smooth while the tree is young. When it matures, the bark becomes rougher. Other pines have deeply fissured bark, making this material very popular for landscape mulch.

All pines come with needles bundled 3 to 5 in a bunch, attached to the stem with a sheath. Cones can be anywhere from 3 inches to 12 inches in length. Some are short and stubby, much like you see as decoration on holiday wreaths. White pinecones are long and tapered. These were the ones Grandma treasured as fire starters for her wood stove. In exchange for gathering buckets of pinecones for her, we could be guaranteed some of her savory chicken pies.

History

The uses of pine in the mundane world are as plentiful as in the magickal world. There is the obvious use of the wood for furniture, houses, and ship building. It was valued for its rapid growth (relative to oak) and its smooth, straight trunks. I don't know where landscapers would be without access to pine needle and pine bark mulch.

The tree yields tar, turpentine, and resins that help preserve other woods. Americans don't often think of pine as a food source, but there is a lot of benefit in pine nuts and the soft inner pine bark.

As the New World opened up, explorers were often keen to settle near stands of pine forests. My own state, North Carolina, exists today because of the vast forests of long-leaf pines that were culled to provide masts for ships; timber for railroads, factories, and furniture; and pine by-products. Up until around the 1860s, North Carolina was the major supplier of these materials.

Uses

I have listed Saturn as the ruler of pine based on the recommendation of Agrippa. However, pine was also favored by other deities. Cybele was said to have turned her lover into a pine after he cheated on her. Dionysus and Bacchus were said to have staffs with pine cones on top. Pine was considered an herb of fertility and courage. Faunus (Pan) also had an affinity for pine. In Ovid's *Fasti*, the poet mentions the worship of Faunus, noting in several instances that his brow is wreathed with pine boughs.[57]

---

57. Ovid, *Fasti*, bk 1., trans. A. S. Kline, Poetry in Translation, 2004, https://www.poetryintranslation.com/PITBR/Latin/OvidFastiBkOne.php.

The Greek Magical Papyri offer this formula for those who wish to be able to copulate a lot. Grind up 50 tiny pinecones with 2 ounces of sweet wine and 2 pepper grains and drink it.[58] Good luck with that. Even if the author of that spell was talking about *P. halepensis* or *P. brutia*, pines likely to have been found in Egypt, that's a whole bunch of ground up pinecones.

Continuing the idea of reproduction, Cupid was frequently depicted wearing a crown of pine boughs. The plant was important to Neptune because ships were made of the rot-resistant pine wood.

While you can use pine in spells for reproduction, for our purposes pine is most often used for health and protection. Pine is a wholesale cleansing, healing herb. There is a reason why pine was considered, until recent years, the most popular fragrance for house-cleaning products. It was frequently used in sick rooms and hospitals. Just as it cleanses, it exorcises. Pine can clear away negativity and ground the user and the area.

CRAFTING: Pine Sap Incense

One look at the resin that oozes from cuts or breaks in the tree and you can see how other popular resins like dragon's blood, frankincense, and myrrh came to be used. You can make your own incense using sap from the pines you find in your area.

As I mentioned when talking about harvesting cherry sap, try not to damage a pine tree to get sap. Find a tree that has been cut or that has been damaged in some way that would cause it to ooze sap. Scrape this into a plastic container.

58. Dieter Betz, ed. *The Greek Magical Papyri in Translation*, 120.

Let's say you want to make a healing incense. First, grind some dried mugwort and plantain to a very fine powder. There ares no exact portions of powdered herb to sap. The amount you will need will depend on how much pine sap you gather and how much moisture it has. I suggest starting with a ½ teaspoon of each dried herb to 1 tablespoon of resin and go from there.

After grinding, set the mixture to one side. Gently warm the sap to make it pliable. You can do this by setting the container of sap in a pot of hot water. Don't get any water in the sap. Think of this as a bain-marie or double boiler.

Once the sap is warm, mash some of the mugwort and plantain powder into the sap using the back of a spoon. Keep adding the herb mixture until the sap begins to get stiff. When you are satisfied with the texture, use the spoon to pinch off a dab of resin about the size of a pea. Put this in the remaining powder and roll it around. At this point, you should be able to use your fingers and not get too sticky.

When the pea feels dry and won't accept any more herb powder, set it aside on a glass plate or metal cookie sheet to finish drying. Keep working until the sap is all used up. If necessary, you might need to roll your incense balls in the dry powder again. Set them on top of the refrigerator or somewhere out of the way for a couple of days to completely dry. Store your incense balls in a tight container and use as needed.

Once you become expert at this technique, you can make incense balls for all kinds of purposes. The only limit is your imagination.

PLANTAIN

Latin Name: *Plantago*

Locations: Lawns, fields

Parts Used: Leaf

Hardiness Zones: 3 to 9

Planetary Ruler: Venus

Uses: Healing, strength, fertility, and protection

Edibility: All plant parts are edible.

Warning: None

Back in the day when I did landscaping for a living, plantain, or *Plantago*, was just another lawn weed. Other than to eradicate it, I never gave plantain another thought.

Appearance

The distinctive ribbed leaves of plantain that Pagans use in magick and medicine form a rosette as soon as temperatures allow it to grow. The leaves can be very broad or very narrow. When the leaves are broad, it is called broadleaf plantain (*P. major*). When they are narrow, it is called ribwort (*P. lanceolata*). *Wort* is just the Old English word for "plant."

Plantain is the bane of the homeowner who takes pride in his or her lawn. Every flower head that plantain throws up contains dozens of seeds, and every seed that is not eaten by critters seems to sprout. They may sprout in a bare spot in the lawn, in a crack in the sidewalk, along the edge of the drive or at the foundation of the house. But given half a chance, they will definitely sprout.

Cutting or mowing a stand of plantain only slows it down for a little bit. The plant soon "learns" to anticipate the weekly trimmings and only hugs the ground that much more closely.

History

Honestly, if you like broadleaf perennials like hostas in the flower bed, a healthy plantain can be quite striking among the flowers. It is drought tolerant. The deer don't seem to be interested in it and not many insect pests bother it. If you keep the seed pods picked off, you've got a free, no-maintenance plant. So far, I haven't been able to convince any homeowners with that argument.

Plantain is listed among the nine sacred herbs of Odin, except there it is called "waybread." The herbs are discussed in a long prayer that has come down to us from before the tenth century. Translated from an herbal work entitled *Lacnunga*, the part about plantain goes like this:

And you waybread
plant mother
eastward open
within mighty
over you chariots creaked
over you queens rode
over you brides trampled
over you oxen snorted
This all you then withstood
and dashed apart
as you withstand
poison and infection
and that evil
that fares through the land[59]

Yes, you can clearly see this is an herb of protection, in the literal and metaphysical sense.

Uses

Herbalists and magick workers have many uses for plantain. The medicinal uses alone could fill a chapter. Most herbalists I know who make salves have some formula of the herb to use for skin ailments. Science shows it is beneficial in some respiratory disorders and for the treatment of colds.[60] Just crushing the leaf and applying the material to a bug bite or a wound can reduce inflammation.

---

59. S. E. S. Eberly, "The Nine Herbs Prayer," Wyrtig, last accessed June 12, 2020, http://www.wyrtig.com/GardenFolklore/NineHerbsPrayer.htm.

60. "Plantain," Drugs.com, last accessed January 23, 2021, https://www.drugs.com/npc/plantain.html.

In magick, Venus governs this plant. It is used for strength, protection, and healing.

It seems to have special wards for travelers. Putting a bit of plantain in the shoe was supposed to make it easy for the traveler to walk miles without tiring.

Beyond that, you don't find many sources that describe a specific magickal use for plantain. In general, it is thought to enhance the power and effect of other herbs in much the same way that dragon's blood resin or frankincense will. With that in mind, you can add dried plantain to any incense for healing or for protection.

When you plan menus around spring rituals, you can add tender young plantain leaves to any salad mix as a way to bring the plant's healing powers to the participants of your ritual. Avoid mature leaves. The fibrous nature and bitter taste of the larger leaves make them less palatable.

Later in the season as the plant makes seed heads, these can be gathered and added to multigrain bread recipes. For this purpose, focus on gathering the long seed pods of *P. major*, the broadleaf plantain, when the seeds have matured to a dark brown or black. You can gather the small heads of ribwort if you have a lot of time to spend on your hands and knees.

CRAFTING: Protective Talisman

Given the plant's reputation for protecting travelers, you can make a simple talisman to carry in your vehicle. On a Tuesday during a waxing moon, gather a small flannel bag or tiny bottle that can be sealed. Harvest and dry a fresh plantain leaf. Chop or grind the leaf to make a fine powder if you are making a bottle charm, or coarsely chop it if you are using a bag.

Add to the container a drawing of the travel rune Raidho. If you would prefer, you can use a sign or symbol of one of the deities known for protecting travelers, such as Hermes, Lord Ganesh, Meili, Xaman Ek, or Khonsu. Small pieces of malachite or moonstone are also good for travel charms.

During your normal ritual, ask your patron deity (deities) to bless your talisman. Hang it in your vehicle or carry it on your person when you travel to help you avoid the common headaches and misfortunes that seem to crop up when you hit the road.

POKE

Latin Name: Phytolacca americana

Locations: Abandoned fields

Parts Used: Berry, root

Hardiness Zone: 4 to 8

Planetary Ruler: Mars

Uses: Breaking hexes, courage, ink (berries)

Edibility: The leaves of poke are edible if boiled
   repeatedly.

Warning: The roots, stems, and berries are considered
   toxic.

Pokeweed is one of my favorite plants to use from the wild
around my home, maybe because it was such a unique part of my
childhood.

Appearance

At a mature height of 6 to 8 feet, it's hard to miss on the side of the road or in abandoned fields. The leaves are pointed ovals of medium green. They start out quite small but can get 12 to 18 inches long and 6 to 10 inches wide at maturity. These come on loose, branching stems that can make poke look like a small tree from a distance. If you miss that, when July and August roll around, shiny clusters of purple berries show up.

History

One of the things I learned from Grandma was how to find and process poke greens in the spring of the year. I know, many resources will tell you that poke is toxic to humans and animals. If that were in fact the case, I would have been dead a long time ago. Not only did we eat cooked poke greens, Grandma insisted we had to eat them. Poke greens, she said, cleaned out all the bad things that had accumulated in the body over the winter. It is true that poke is a purgative: it will ensure you use the toilet—regularly. Now that I think about it, all the pork grease she cooked them in probably had something to do with that too.

That's not to say Grandma didn't teach me some "dos and don'ts" when it came to picking and processing poke. These are still very important. Although people have eaten and continue to eat poke, it is imperative that you process it correctly.

I was told never to pick leaves greater than 6 inches long or the resulting side dish would make us sick. That wasn't exactly true. You can't send little ten-to-twelve-year-old kids out with a big paper bag, tell them to fill it up before they can go play, and expect them not to take some shortcuts. We fudged on the size of the leaves, naturally. Somehow, they got cooked up and we ate them anyway.

Another golden rule is you don't pick poke greens after it sets berries. I have, on occasion as an adult, violated this rule too. So far, it hasn't killed me.

Finally, poke greens have to be boiled in fresh water three different times before they are edible. This is a definite inviolable rule. In addition to boiling the leaves in three different batches of fresh water, Mama and Grandma would sauté the greens in a large iron skillet of bacon or fatback grease for about 20 minutes before adding 6 to 10 scrambled eggs. If you ever wondered how to make poke salad (sallet), there you go.

The substances in poke that are considered toxic are oxalic acid, saponins, and an alkaloid. These substances are present in immature leaves, from which they can be boiled out. You cannot do that with the berries or the root.

Don't even think about ingesting berries or roots of the poke plant. No amount of boiling will protect you from bad effects if you eat berries off the plant or munch on a root. The root has some naturopathic uses but only in the hands of a skilled, trained naturopath. To be totally, completely safe, don't eat mature leaves from the plant. Don't harvest leaves greater than 6 inches long. And, by all means, never, never eat leaves that haven't been boiled multiple times to remove any possible toxins.

Uses

Poke is easy to find in abandoned fields, easements, and waste areas, especially in the South. As mentioned earlier, the root can be used in banishing or hexing magick. Roots can be very hard to dig up. The taproot is massive in a mature plant and bores deep into the ground. I have never had a problem with handling the root, but as pointed out earlier, the root is the main reservoir of pokeweed toxics. If you are worried, wear gloves before handling it.

Because it is so fibrous, the root should be cut up into small pieces prior to drying. Otherwise, you might need a bandsaw to cut the whole dried root into usable pieces. The root can be used in any spell or recipe for hexing or protection. I have used it as a replacement for dragon's blood resin to add energy to spellwork.

CRAFTING: Pokeweed Magickal Ink

Pokeweed berries can be used to make a magickal ink. You can find plenty of recipes for making poke ink on the internet. Many will tell you to mash 2 cups of the berries, strain the juice, and add roughly 1 teaspoon of white vinegar.

You can certainly do that. A friend of mine has inherited letters from an ancestor who fought in the Civic War. Some of those letters were written in pokeberry ink. He tells me soldiers would sharpen a stick, gather a lot of berries, stab the berries with the stick and write their letters. The letters are faded but still legible.

I simmer the berries (stems and all) in an iron pot for at least 6 hours with just enough water to cover the plant material, strain the juice, and toss the remaining berries. I put the liquid back in the pot and simmer the juice until it has a thick enough consistancy to work on a quill. At that point, I add 1 crushed vitamin C tablet per cup of liquid for preservation and store in a sealed jar in a cool area for later use.

The ink is ready to use for any purpose, be that for spells, journaling, or recording items in your Book of

Shadows. I've even had one local artist tell me he uses it in his painting because he loves the color.

You can also use pokeberry ink as a base to make dragon's blood, dove's blood, and bat's blood inks. Add ½ ounce of dragon's blood essential oil to 7 ounces of pokeberry ink for dragon's blood ink. Bat's blood ink can be made with 7 ounces of pokeberry ink, ¼ ounce of myrrh essential oil, and ¼ ounce of cinnamon oil. Dove's blood is a mix of 7 ounces of pokeberry ink, ¼ ounce each of cinnamon essential oil, rose or rose geranium essential oil, and dragon's blood essential oil.

Dove's blood ink can be made with cherries as well. Simply follow the same instructions for juicing and then reducing the cherries. Add the same essential oils.

All these inks should last a long time in small containers. If you would like to be sure, store them in the refrigerator between uses. Expect organic inks to fade a bit with time, especially if the paper is regularly exposed to sunlight. This will not be a problem for spell writing. However, it may require touching up writings in your Book of Shadows periodically.

SWEET GUM

Latin Name: Liquidamber styraciflua

Locations: Landscape, forest

Parts Used: Burr, sap

Hardiness Zones: 5 to 9

Planetary Ruler: Sun

Uses: Exorcism, protection, spell breaking, and increasing the power of other herbs

Edibility: All parts of sweet gum are considered nontoxic.

Warning: None

Sweet gum is a tree that homeowners and landscape maintenance people love to hate. It is adored for its sturdiness, broad, shading canopy, and beautiful fall foliage. But it is hated for its seed pods.

Appearance

Sweetgum, or *Liquidamber,* seedpods begin to fall late in the year. The full Latin name for our American sweetgum is *Liquidamber styraciflua.* This tree can get 60 to 80 feet tall on average, but 100-foot tall specimens are not unusual. While it is a deciduous tree that loses its leaves in the fall, those leaves have a glossy look that might deceive you into thinking it is an evergreen. The leaves form almost perfect star shapes roughly the size of an adult's hand.

History

A common name for trees in this genus is storax. In fact, one of the less well-known names for sweet gum is American storax. Why is this of interest?

Storax has been used since ancient times in perfumes and incense. It was thought to purify the air of negative influences and was especially valued for love spells and amorous activities. You can still get *L. orientalis* (Turkish sweetgum) as an oil or resin, but it is pricey and not easy to come by. I don't advocate harming the tree to harvest the sap, but if I should happen by a tree that has been cut down or that has a weeping wound, I would not pass this treasure by.

As is not uncommon in the plant kingdom, some confusion exists between styrax and storax. *Styrax benzoin,* or benzoin, as it is commonly sold, is not the same thing as storax. For one thing, storax is richly fragrant; bezoin smells of vanilla but is more often used as a fixative for other fragrances. Both can be used for protection, but benzoin is not used in love spells.

Uses

The burrs, or witch's balls, are what Pagans use from this sun herb to protect against evil and for banishing. Some believe that just having the burrs on the altar during a spell lends great power to the magickal work being done.

CRAFTING: Banishing Spell 2

I have a rather involved spell for banishing problems (or people) that is based on the use of sweet gum burrs. It requires time and effort, but I find it to be most effective. If you do several at a time, you can store the extras for later use.

I assemble them in the waning moon at my altar after setting appropriate wards. The burrs are dipped in a beeswax that has equal amounts boneset, clove, and frankincense mixed into it. The boneset is to ward off negativity, the clove drives away hostile energy and purifies, and the frankincense uplifts the person and drives away negative energy.

In a separate blend, I mix an incense of hyssops, heliotrope, salt, frankincense, and knotweed. This is put into a bag. After dipping each burr in the candle wax, I toss it into the bag and shake it up. Repeat until all burrs are covered with the dried herb mix. The hyssop cleanses, the heliotrope exorcises and heals, the salt purifies and grounds, frankincense uplifts the person and drives away negative energy, and the knotweed binds the problem to the token.

The burrs are then placed in a clean bag or cloth pouch, wrapped in a black cloth, and left on my altar for just over

24 hours. After 24 hours, I again set up the altar with the appropriate wards. Then I light a black candle along with frankincense incense. As I pass each burr through the candle flame and smoke, I chant:

Hyssops, heliotrope, salt of the plains
Frankincense, knotweed banish my pain
Harm no one while at this task
But by all powers, make it last
That which plagues me, make it go
Burned or buried, now make it so

I chant this over and over while I pass each burr through the flame and the smoke. I store the burrs until I need one or until someone requests one.

When it comes time to use the burr, the petitioner should wait, if possible, for a waning moon. Hold the burr in the dominant hand and visualize the problem moving into the charm. Hold tightly but don't try to crush; the discomfort should represent the problem.

Call on a favorite deity and chant, "This problem I can no longer stand. I see it clearly in my hand."

Once you can no longer hold a clear focus on the problem, the charm must be immediately buried or burned.

To bury: Find an out-of-the-way spot in the landscape. Dig a hole and drop the burr in. Take a few moments to meditate on the hole consuming the charm plus the problem. (Suggested chant: *My problem I will no longer miss.* *Now I put an end to this.*) Cover. Stand and stomp the dirt over the hole. That symbolizes control over and the end of the problem.

To burn: Place the burr in a cauldron or fireproof dish. Light it. As it burns, see the problem being consumed. Use the chant suggested in the burying method. The charm should burn for about 10 to 20 minutes. Let it burn out on its own. Immediately discard the ashes by flushing them down the toilet, burying them in the landscape, or dropping them into a running stream or river.

As with all magick, the petitioner should be working on addressing the problem in the real world too.

THISTLE

Latin Name: Carduus, Centaurea benedicta, Silybum

Locations: Fields, gardens

Parts Used: Leaf

Hardiness Zones: 3 to 9

Planetary Ruler: Mars

Uses: Exorcism, hex breaking, healing, and purification

Edibility: These are nontoxic.

Warning: None

Thistle is a Mars herb, as you might suspect when you see the abundant prickles that cover the leaves of the plant. Look for thistles in pastures and easements. A few are grown as ornamentals in the cottage garden. There are a variety of thistles—Scotch, milk, holy, and so on—that fall into several plant genera, such as *Carduus* and *Centaurea*.

Appearance

The flower of the thistle is typically a soft pink, lavender, or purple tuft of tubular petals held tight by a spiny head of bracts. The leaves can be a rich green, waxy, and thick or dull green, unwaxed, and thin. The spines are present on most leaves but are more prominent on some varieties of thistles than others. Some thistles are biennial; others are perennial.

History

The most iconic thistle is perhaps the Scottish thistle, which may be a musk thistle (*Carduus nutans*) or lady thistle (*Silybum marianum*). Lady thistle is also known as milk thistle, owing to the white splotches on its spiny leaves. Some sources list *Onopordon acanthium* as the real Scotch thistle.

Either way, it is the national emblem of the country. Legend has it that invading Norse hordes sneaking into the country from the sea at night stepped on the spiny plant and gave away their intentions with their cries of pain. This, in addition to the mere presence of thorns, lends to the plant's reputation for protection.

You may have heard your grandparents cursing sow thistle as they weeded their vegetable patch. This isn't a true thistle; it is in the dandelion tribe of plants, specifically in the genus *Sonchus*. The form of the plant is similar to true thistle with large, irregularly lobed leaves bearing ragged edges, but the flower head is yellow and ragged points on the leaves are not spiny.

Sow thistle isn't sacred to Mars. It is sacred to Hecate and ruled by Venus. Gathering it to honor either deity would be appropriate.

As with all other plants I have spoken of, there are look-alikes in the landscape too. In this case, the confusion is natural. The word *thistle* was originally not considered to be a plant classification so much as a description of any spiny plant with globe-like flower head. When you read about thistles in some spell books, old and new, they may be talking about teasels (*Dipsacus*), eryngos (*Eryngium*), or globe thistles (*Echinops*).

Uses

The uses for thistle are many. In addition to being useful for honoring Mars, the plant can be burned to strengthen the vim and vigor of the men in your life. Guys who eat Carline thistle are said to gain the sexual potency of a stallion. However, the herb has to be planted and harvested at the stroke of midnight under a new Moon.

Old herbalists used to cure everything from fever to worms with thistle. This is where the plant gets a reputation for healing.

Any plant with stickers, spines, or briars can be used in hexing or cursing, and the same is true of thistle. This one comes with a strong Christian influence. Thistle was among the plants God was said to populate the earth with in order to punish Adam for his sin. Practitioners use the dried leaves to stuff poppets used for baneful purpose, in part, for this reason.

On the other hand, Dioscorides prescribed the plant's root as a solution to melancholy, if carried. You see a primary truth in magick as in life: that which can protect can also harm and vice versa.

CRAFTING: Warding Ritual

I hope, as magick practitioners, you regularly ward your-self and the place where you live. Thistle offers you a way to do this. This can be done anytime you feel the need. However, you should regularly ward yourself once a lunar cycle in a waning moon.

For yourself, you can draw a warm bath to which you have added a handful of thistle and mimosa. Light a black candle and burn frankincense as you soak in the herb bath. If you like, you can do as they do in some African and Carribbean traditions and put a fresh egg in the bath with you. When you have soaked away any negative ener-gies, drain the bath. Take the herbs and the egg outdoors and bury them, preferably away from your home. If you happen to live in an apartment, take the material directly to the dumpster.

To rid your home of negativity and prevent it from seeping in, brew a floor wash with thistle and mimosa. A handful of each herb will be enough, added to a quart of boiling water. Let the herbs steep for 10 to 15 minutes. Strain and add the tea to your mop water. Clean as you normally do.

When you are done, you can pour the water around the perimeter of your home if possible. If that isn't possi-ble, use the leftover water to asperge your doorways.

VIOLET

Latin Name: Viola

Locations: Lawns, flower gardens

Parts Used: Flower

Hardiness Zones: 3 to 8

Planetary Ruler: Venus

Uses: Love, night magick, virtue, peace, lust, broken
hearts, and healing

Edibility: All parts are edible.

Warning: None

Appearance

Violets are easy to spot in the lawn or on the roadside. They have
rather large, heart-shaped leaves that remain evergreen in all but

the most northerly climates. Violets bloom in cool weather, most abundantly in late winter and early spring but sporadically in fall. My yard is so littered with white and blue violet blossoms at this time that it looks like a ticker-tape parade has rolled through.

All violet flowers have five petals suspended on a delicate stem that forms a bit of a shepherd's hook on which to hang its flower. Violets can be white, blue, pale blue, lavender, dark purple, yellow, and pink, although those last two colors aren't often seen in the average landscape. If you have tried to dig out violets from the lawn, you have probably noticed the plant has a thick, knotty root. This tough root is one of the reasons why spraying herbicide to kill violets takes several applications.

All pansies (*Viola* ×*wittrockiana*) are violets, but not all violets are pansies. These are the colorful biennials that come in all the colors of the rainbow, plus a few colors that aren't seen in the rainbow, like black. You instantly recognize this popular landscape flower by its "face." The face is formed by the dark splotches or blotches on four of the five colorful petals.

If your pansies don't have faces, they are still *Viola* ×*wittrockiana*. However, these are known in the trade as "clear" pansies. Most homeowners like the large flowers of the face pansy, but the smaller pansies show up in garden centers too. These are often *V. tricolor,* or what your grandmother might have called Johnny-jump-ups. In Europe, they are more often called heartsease.

If you can't find wild violets in the lawn, look for pansies in container gardens or mass plantings in the spring and fall.

One thing you can't substitute for violas is the houseplant African violet (*Saintpaulia*). Mama's fascination for sweet violas eventually lead her to become quite an accomplished grower of African violets. But these two plants have nothing in common other than vaguely similar flowers.

History

When I first began writing garden columns and researching plants, my mother had a simple request. Could I please find her some sweet violets for her yard? One of her favorite movies was *My Fair Lady*, with Audrey Hepburn in the title role in 1964 as Eliza Dolittle. As a street urchin, Eliza sold violets to obtuse London socialites to make a meager living. Mama so wanted to be able to pick her own sweet violets. That bit of theater was based on real history. Selling flowers, especially sweet-smelling violets, was often a way for rural folks to earn money from more well-heeled patrons in the city.

Sadly, I was never able to find true sweet violets, or *Viola odorata,* for Mama while she was alive. I did try. I scoured nurseries and garden centers. But with so many people trying to eradiate the common wild violets (*V. sororia,* syn. *V. papilionacea,* or *V. palustris*) from their lawns, garden centers were not the least bit interested in offering a fragrant version of the plant.

I also tried mail-order catalogs. The few plants I received and planted for my mother never offered up the least whiff of fragrance. This was several decades ago. I can only hope online vendors have gotten more reputable than their mail-order cousins.

Uses

Some say Saturn rules this herb; others say Venus. Either way, violets are used in love spells and charms. If you come across the ingredient ionone in some of the old grimiores, that's the old word for violets.

Use the flowers in spells for honesty, humility, healing, and wishes. Mix carefully with lavendar to promote lust. If you want to soften the hard heart of a person in your life, use violets in your magick.

I mentioned earlier that one name for violet is heartsease. Different sources give different reasons for the name. Some say it comes from the satisfaction one gets from simply gazing at the flower. Focusing on the unassuming beauty of the plant in bloom is thought to take one's mind off the hecticness of life, if only for a little while.

Others point to the medicinal use of the leaves in tea that can take away anxiety. Collect the leaves from plants that you know have not been treated with any pesticides. Dry them under low heat. Add 1 tablespoon of minced dried leaves to 16 ounces of boiling water and remove the water from the heat source. Strain after 10 minutes and drink. You can add 1 tablespoon of lavender to the tea for extra effect. Sweeten to taste. The drink is not sedating but should calm your anxious heart.

CRAFTING: Love Spray

The name *heartsease* may also have to do with the plant's attribution for love. It is said to help draw love to you. And when love goes and breaks your heart, violet can help you feel better. I make a spray by mixing together 3 allspice seeds, 6 drops of dragon's blood essential oil, and 12 drops of violet essential oil in a blend of 8 ounces of water and 8 ounces of vodka. I also include some dried violet flowers or leaves if I don't have fresh flowers. The allspice is for healing, the dragon's blood is for courage to face our sorrow, and the violet is to ease the pain in our heart.

This should be combined in a waning moon and allowed to infuse for at least 2 weeks before use. For added effect, you can call on an appropriate deity, such as Venus, Kwan Yin, or Isis, for assistance in blessing the mixture. Spray the solution on bed pillows and on clothing to subtly help you find your way back from a broken heart.

WALNUT

Latin Name: *Juglans nigra*

Locations: Forest

Parts Used: Wood, nut

Hardiness Zones: 5 to 9

Planetary Ruler: Sun

Uses: Blessings, health, infertility, and mental powers

Edibility: The nuts are edible.

Warning: None

Walnut trees have long been associated with witches, who were once thought to favor the trees to dance under in the moonlight. Black walnut (*Juglans nigra*) is the most common walnut tree in the wild in the United States.

Appearance

It's hard to miss when the dull green, odorous nuts begin to fall late in the season. It's even harder to miss when the green husks come off and homeowners are left with a persistent black stain on their decks or driveways.

The tree itself can get quite large. It has a loose canopy with simple, pointed oval leaves, 7 to 9 arranged along a single stem. Springtime allergy sufferers know when the tree is in bloom, as it causes them quite some problem for several weeks. You don't have to live near a walnut tree to suffer its effects. The wind will do an excellent job of carrying the pollen to your doorstep.

History

In Europe, wildcrafters would have looked for *J. regia*. Americans call it English walnut. Europeans call it Persian walnut after its general region of origin. The tree is prized for its wood, its oil, and its nuts as a food source. In particular, Europeans seem to make a variety of foods out of walnuts, from pickles to liquor. Of course, Americans are dealing with black walnuts, and there is a significant difference in the taste.

But it is in Italy where the walnut tree gets its reputation as a familiar to witches. In Italian folklore as recounted by the nineteenth century author Charles Leland, the goddess Aradia was born to mortal parents after her earthbound mother ate some walnuts from a tree in the town of Benevento. Shortly thereafter, the woman discovered she was pregnant. The child was allegedly a blessing from the goddess Diane and the god Apollo. Called Arabella by her mundane parents, she grew to become a protector of witches and other common folks. After fleeing to the woods near the town, she took the name Aradia, and after a long time on earth, she eventually returned to her place among the gods.

In time, the town of Benevento became known as the Town of the Witches. It is located in the center of the Italian penisula, roughly thirty miles north of Naples and 130 miles south of Rome. Even during the time of Roman occupation (400 to 300 BCE), the town was known for its worship of Isis. The locals later became attached to Diane and Hecate.

By the Middle Ages, witches were believed to be everywhere in the countryside. They pranked farmers by matting the manes of their horses and souring the cow's milk. When they gathered, the witches were thought to dance wildly around a special walnut tree, raising spirits and cavorting with the devil. They arrived onsite using a flying ointment, the recipe for which Diane allegedly taught them. Local citizens thought the witches would rub the ointment on their chest, chanting the following:

Unguent, unguent,
Carry me to the walnut tree of Benevento
Above the water and above the wind
And above all other bad weather.[61]

Keep in mind, this story comes to us from Christian sources and may be subject to embellishment. Mr. Leland is also believed to have spiced up his stories with a bit of imagination.

Uses

Since you aren't likely to come by *J. regia* here in the States, I will be talking about the black walnut. All walnuts are sun herbs. This

---

61. Craig Spencer, *Aradia: A Modern Guide to Charles Godfrey Leland's Gospel of the Witches* (Woodbury, MN: Llewellyn Publications, 2020), 107.

is a bit unusual because the European walnut was originally considered to be sacred to Jupiter, a sky not sun deity; the nuts were even called colloquially Jove's nuts. But Sun or Jupiter, the walnut tree is a positive herb that can give today's witch a number of valuable supplies.

The nuts are used for wishes, health, and mental agility. A spell you will see frequently in books of the occult is to place a wish inside the empty hulls of a walnut and bury it. Most often, the writer will illustrate this using an English walnut, but you can also use black walnuts. That is, assuming you can get the hull cleanly open.

My grandmother loved black walnut pound cake. One way to gain her favor was to volunteer to crack enough black walnuts to get a couple of cups of nut meats for her. We had a lot of fun wailing on those black walnut hulls with a hammer. But trying to cleave them neatly in half was a futile labor. Most often, we pounded the bejezus out of them and scraped up the pulverized meats.

CRAFTING: Walnut Magickal Ink

The messy skin of a black walnut will yield an excellent ink. Get a pair of gloves. Walnuts make a very persistant stain on anything they touch. You might also want to wear something you won't mind throwing away if you have an accident and splash the stain onto your clothing.

Take 12 ripe walnuts with skins that have begun to turn black. Put them in a heavy metal pot and add enough water to cover the nuts. Bring to a boil, then reduce the heat to simmer the nuts. Cook on a low simmer for 12 hours. Turn off the heat and let the nuts sit for another 12 hours. You can use a crock pot for the simmering. However, it is best to bring the nuts and the liquid to a good rolling boil to start.

When the liquid is ready, strain the solids away through cheesecloth. Reduce the remaining liquid by about half by simmering it until done. Cool the liquid. Add 1 tablespoon of vinegar to help preserve the ink and up to 1 tablespoon of gum arabic if your ink isn't thick enough.

Store in dark glass bottles if you can. This will help preserve the color longer. Sunlight has a tendency to break down natural inks. In addition to writing with your ink, you can use it to stain any wooden tools like wands or staffs.

WILLOW

Latin Name: *Salix*

Locations: Landscape, forest

Parts Used: Leaf, wood

Hardiness Zones: 4 to 10

Planetary Ruler: Moon

Uses: Love, love divination, spirit work, funeral rites,
   moon magick, and healing

Edibility: All parts are nontoxic.

Warning: None

What better plant to follow the walnut tree with than willow
(*Salix*)? Willow is a moon herb and associated with all things
feminine.

Appearance

The image people tend to associate with willow is the weeping willow (*S. babylonica*). These trees can be found all over the country. If you're looking for willow in the wild in the United States, you are more likely to find black willow (*S. nigra*). This is not a reference to good and bad. Black willows are called black because of the dark fissured bark. In Europe, the wild willow is *S. alba*, the white willow.

You don't see them in the landscape so much anymore, but pussy willows (*S. discolor*) are attractive shrub-form willows. Cultivated varieties display gray, silver, or pink fuzzy pods just before the flowers open. If you have one in your landscape, feel free to use it as a substitute for any working that calls for willow.

Willows are among the first trees to leaf out in spring. All tree-form willows have long, narrow lance-shaped leaves. Home-owners will occasionaly become frustrated with the tree because of its habit of dropping little stems all through the year. It is a messy tree. However, that can be a boon for those of us looking to gather material for our spellwork.

You find willow trees in damp places, often along river and stream banks or low wet areas. The trees and shrubs have extensive root systems that make the tree difficult to remove, if someone is ever tempted to try. When the tree is cut, it's not unusual to see sprouts return from the base at the first opportunity.

History

Willow has an association among mundanes as a tree of sadness and bad luck. My brother-in-law certainly ascribes to this notion. My sister loves willows. Everywhere she and her husband moved to, one of her first improvements was to add a weeping willow to the property. After the third move, her husband forbid her to plant another one, claiming every time she did and the tree really got to growing, his job required him to move or an irresistible career change presented itself. They eventually ended up in an arid part of Texas that would not support a willow without considerable effort. My sister could not wait to move back to North Carolina. The compromise was they'd move back and she'd stop planting willows.

Raymond Buckland pointed out in *The Witch Book* that the willow gained a depressing reputation in the Middle Ages when Christian writers ascribed all kinds of misery and suffering to it.[62] Buckland was a leading figure in the 1970s when interest in Wicca and Paganism was at an all-time high. He was a prolific writer on occult and spiritual matters.

In Christian traditions, it was said Christ was whipped with willow branches on his way to the cross, causing the tree to forever bend or weep in regret. Other writers said the tree gave up its upright habit on learning of the death of Christ, choosing instead to weep for the world's loss.

Shakespeare didn't do the tree any favors, using it frequently as a prop for forelorn lovers or people who had been driven mad from saddess. The British, never ones to let a dark metaphor go to waste, were wont to describe someone in mourning as "wearing the willow." The earliest reference to the term that I can find is from *The Literary Panorama*, volume 14, published in 1813. This was a compilation of book, play, and article reviews of the time. Editor Charles Taylor quotes a text from 1723: "Huntingdonshire is a very proper county for unseccessful lovers to live

---

62. Raymond Buckland, *The Witch Book: The Encyclopedia of Witchcraft, Wicca, and Neo-paganism* (Canton, MI: Visible Ink Press, 2002), 517.

in; for, upon the loss of their sweethearts, they will here find an abundance of Willow-trees, so that they may either *wear the willow green,* or hang themselves, which they please: but the latter is reckoned the best remedy for slighted love."[63] A bit of a harsh perspective, if you ask me. Mr. Taylor does write in the same article that the general association of willows and sorrow was very commonplace.

European folklore is filled with stories of some fellow who encounters and eventually marries the lovely spirit of a willow tree. They live happily and start a family until, inevitably in every story, the fool goes and cuts down the willow tree. Sometimes he is tricked into doing it. Other times, he develops the idea that he can keep his bride with him forever if her link to nature is severed. Either way, she ends up dead or forever gone. The poor kid who is left behind can only be consoled by being given a cradle made of the fallen willow wood and rocking in his mother's aboreal arms.

Of course, Pagan traditions also allude to a rather sad history for the tree. Circe was said to have a grove of willows whose branches were festooned with corpses. A grove to Persephone, Queen of Hades, was made up of black poplars and willows. Even Orpheus carried a willow branch with him as he descended to Hades on a failed mission to retrieve his lover.

Uses

What can I do to reclaim this poor girl's image? Well, for starters, it's not all bad for the willow in every tradition. The Chinese see the bowing willow as a sign of humility, not sorrow. The

---

63. *The Literary Panorama Being a Compendium of National Papers and Parliamentary Reports, Illustrative of the History, Statistics, and Commerce of the Empire,* vol. 14., ed. Charles Taylor (London: Cox and Baylis, 1813), 730.

tree is considered a symbol of immortality and rebirth. This is particularly appropriate for this tree. Long before the advent of plant growth hormones, gardeners would gather a bucket full of fresh willow stems and leaves. They would cover the material with water and let it sit in the sun for a couple of days. The water would then be used to root cuttings and to help new plant sets to develop roots. I can personally vouch for this technique.

Willow wood is used to make wands. The Celtic goddess Brigit is said to carry a wand of white willow. Offering baskets as well as baskets for mundane purposes were frequently woven of flexible willow stems. Having a vase of willow stems on the altar as a tribute to any moon goddess would certainly be appreciated.

Medieval writers may have distorted the original purpose of willows. Far from being a totem for lost love, in witchcraft, the leaves and bark are used for love spells and healing, especially healing sorrow. You will recall I said earlier that violet, or heartsease, can be used to mend a broken heart. Combining violet and willow in an incense is another way to help those who suffer from an emotional heartache.

Willow is among the nine sacred trees required for a Celtic balefire at Beltain and Samhain. The others are birch, hazel, holly, oak, alder, ash, hawthorn, and rowan. If you use the Celtic Ogham alphabet for scrying, the symbols can be marked on willow wood for divination. Scott Cunningham recommends mixing powdered willow bark and sandlewood and burning it at the waning moon to conjure spirits.[64]

Because of its association with water, dowsing sticks are made of willow. Quite appropriately, these tools are also called witching rods. I've only known one person who could successfully dowse.

---

64. Cunningham, *Cunningham's Encyclopedia of Magical Herbs*, 250.

He was a little obnoxious to be around and more than a little "touched in the head," as my grandmother would have said, so I never asked him to train me in the practice.

CRAFTING: Creativity Incense and Spell

Willows are also considered sources of inspiration for poets and musicians. Lingering under the tree, watching the water of a river or stream float by can induce a state of wakeful dreaming in which the universe or patron deities can reach out with inspiration. If someone has ever asked you for help to spur on their creative process, making an incense of equal portions willow, mint, and rosemary would be a good way to get them started. The mixture should be burned at their work station or prior to going to bed at night.

Put a little extra incense powder in a gris-gris bag along with some stones that are helpful for artists like moonstone, tiger's eye, and blue agate. You do the same thing with a small witch bottle that can be suspended from a cord or chain. In place of the large stone, use small chips from one or more of the stones listed above. This should be recharged nightly when they burn the incense for continuing inspiration.

Conclusion

So, here we are, a few hours after we met on that park bench in the introduction, at the end of our discussion on wildcrafting.

You should have a better understanding of why we use plants in general and local plants specifically to achieve our magickal and spiritual goals. If you are new to this Pagan world, I hope you have found in this book a good resource on which to build your studies going forward. If you are an experienced Pagan of any tradition and have been around the cauldron, so to speak, for a few years, I hope you have found a supplemental resource that you can use from time to time.

Before we say goodbye, let me touch very briefly on the subject of spirituality. You may have noticed that I don't give a lot of direction in this book on what spirituality is or how you should approach your own spirituality. This book focuses on magickal practices, not spiritual development. It is not my place to tell you how you should grow spiritually. That is between you and the Divine, however you perceive the Divine.

But I don't want you to go away with the misunderstanding that the essence of being Pagan is practicing magick. In my opinion, that would put you on par with the puffers of alchemy.

Alchemy is the art of transformation in concert with nature and is variously called the Great Art or the Great Work.[65] Sincere practitioners of alchemy have as their goal spiritual development and improvement. They achieve this through meditation and practical applications, the coincidental result of which in some cases is said to be gold, the immortal metal. Some believe gold in this case is a metaphor for the ultimate improvement of the soul; others believe its outcome is really gold. Those who practiced alchemy simply to create gold were called "puffers." It's a reference to the bellows and firing process used while changing base metals into gold. Puffers were interested in alchemy for the benefits they could achieve in the mundane world. They didn't care for spiritual development.[66]

People who pick up an occult book with the goal of causing someone to love them or forcing a boss to give them a promotion they may or may not deserve fall into this category, in my opinion. Pagans whose only involvement in the occult is doing magick are just a couple steps away from that classification—again, in my opinion.

As I have said repeatedly throughout this book, the intention of getting you involved with wildcrafting is to help you become more connected with the universe. You are not master of the universe. You are a part of the universe. Understanding your place in the universe can help you improve your situation here and bring you greater peace.

As you participate in the universe, gathering material to use either for magickal works or spiritual honorings, you can begin

---

65. Dennis William Hauck, *Sorcerer's Stone: A Beginner's Guide to Alchemy* (New York: Citadel Press, 2004), 6.

66. Hauck, *Sorcerer's Stone*, 36.

to relate to this connectivity that Pagans call the Web of Life or the World Web.

You do this by treating your environment with respect. You communicate with the plants around you as you collect your material, and you thank those plants for their contribution to your work. You give back to that environment by leaving offerings in exchange for what you take. To the degree that you have control over some part of your corner of the universe, you act as a good steward. In doing so, you should begin to feel a sense of humility and appreciation for your place in the universe.

And you should do this daily. You may not gather herbs for workings on a daily basis, but you can connect with the universe on a daily basis. When I walk my dog past the yews that frame the entrance to my yard, I often reach out to stroke their rich, green, soft foliage and say, "Hi, babies. How are you doing today?"

I like yews. They are sacred to Hecate, my patron deity. Since Hecate is the deity of entrance ways and crossroads, planting yews at the symbolic boundary between my home and the outside world felt right. When I reach out to touch the yews, I am also reaching out to touch my patron.

When I go to the garden to harvest tomatoes or lettuce or whatever is in season, I rarely pluck a vegetable without saying thank you or asking the plant how it is doing. Of course, I am also inspecting the plant to see if it is experiencing any problems with insects or disease or if it needs water or fertilizer. If you're not actively managing your garden, you're just the crazy lady at the end of the road carrying on one-sided conversations with the green things growing there, in my mind.

As you get comfortable connecting to the plants around you, you should also find it easy to see your connection to your deities. As the hawk circles over my home on its daily patrols, I stop to look in its direction and say, "Hello, Father God. Thanks for looking out for me today." Late in the evening as I end my chores or go from the truck to the house, I look up to see where the moon is. When I see her, I say, "Hello, Mother Goddess. It's been a busy day today. Thanks for watching over me." From my perspective, I'm not just seeing a flying bird or a huge hunk of rock in space. I am seeing embodiments of the Divine in its male and female aspects. This is what I mean when I encourage you to make a connection with the universe.

Hopefully, I've helped you gain a better appreciation of your own environment. I hope you'll view your neighborhood with new eyes. I can imagine that the boring drive to work will now take on new meaning as you watch for plants along the roadside that can help you with your magical journey. I'll bet you'll never walk down a city street or through a parking lot again without noticing what is growing, flowering, or just plain surviving all around you. Keeping learning. Keep growing. Keep experimenting. Make that connection and reap the benefits in your life.

Bibliography

Agrippa, Henry Cornelius. *Three Books of Occult Philosophy.*
Translated by James Freake. Edited by Donald Tyson. St. Paul,
MN: Llewellyn Publications, 2004.

Bennett, Bradley C. "Doctrine of Signatures: An Explanation of
Medicinal Plant Discovery or Dissemination of Knowledge?"
Economic Botany 61, no. 3 (2007): 246–55. www.jstor.org
/stable/4257221.

Bible. New International Version. Biblica, 2011. www.bibleref
.com.

The Book of the Sacred Magic of Abramelin the Mage. Translated
by S. L. MacGregor Mathers. New York: Dover Publications,
1975.

Buckland, Raymond. *The Witch Book: The Encyclopedia of
Witchcraft, Wicca, and Neo-paganism.* Canton, MI: Visible
Ink Press, 2002.

Crowley, Aleister. *Magick in Theory and Practice: Part III of Book
Four.* New York: Castle Books, 1929.

Cunningham, Scott. *Cunningham's Encyclopedia of Magical
Herbs.* St. Paul, MN: Llewellyn Publications, 2001.

Dieter Betz, Hans, ed. *The Greek Magical Papyri in Translation, Including the Demotic Spells*. 2nd ed. Chicago: University of Chicago Press, 1993.

Dioscorides. *De Materia Medica: Being an Herbal with Many Other Medicinal Materials, Written in Greek in the First Century of the Common Era*. Translated by T. A. Osbaldeston and R. P. A. Wood. Johannesburg: Ibidis Press, 2000.

Ellacombe, Henry N. *The Plant-Lore & Garden-Craft of Shakespeare*. London: Edward Arnold, 1896. Reprint, Dover Publications, 2017.

Folkard, Robert. *Plant Lore, Legends, and Lyrics*. London: R. Folkard and Son, 1884.

Fortune, Dion. "The Rationale of Magic." *London Forum* 60, no. 3 (September 1934): 175–81.

Grieve, Maud. *A Modern Herbal*. 2 vols. New York: Harcourt, Brace & Co., 1931. Reprint, Dover Publications, 1971.

Guthrie, W. K. C. *The Greek Philosophers from Thales to Aristotle*. New York: Harper Perennial, 1975.

Hauck, Dennis William. *Sorcerer's Stone: A Beginner's Guide to Alchemy*. New York: Citadel Press, 2004.

Kraig, Donald Michael. *Modern Magick: Eleven Lessons in the High Magickal Arts*. St. Paul, MN: Llewellyn Publications, 1993.

The Literary Panorama Being a Compendium of National Papers and Parliamentary Reports, Illustrative of the History, Statistics, and Commerce of the Empire. Vol. 14. Edited by Charles Taylor. London: Cox and Baylis, 1813.

MacCulloch, J. A. *The Religion of the Ancient Celts*. Edinburgh, UK: T&T Clark, 1911.

Magika Hiera: Ancient Greek Magic and Religion. Edited by Christopher A. Faraone and Dirk Obbink. New York: Oxford University Press, 1997.

McCoy, Edain. *Making Magick: What It Is and How It Works.* St. Paul, MN: Llewellyn Publications, 1997.

McHoy, Peter. *Anatomy of a Garden.* New York: Gallery Books, 1987.

Ovid. *Fasti.* Bk 1. Translated by A. S. Kline. Poetry in Translation, 2004. https://www.poetryintranslation.com/PITBR /Latin/Fastihome.php.

Pliny the Elder. *Natural History.* Translated by John Bostock and H. T. Riley. London: Henry G. Bohn, 1855. http://www .perseus.tufts.edu/hopper/text?doc=Perseus:text:1999.02.0137.

Porcher, Francis Peyre. *Resources of Southern Fields and Forests, Medical, Economical and Agricultural: Being Also a Medical Botany of the Confederate States, with Practical Information on Useful Properties of the Trees, Plants, and Shrubs.* Richmond, VA: West and Johnson, 1863.

Reade, W. Winwood. *The Veil of Isis, or The Mysteries of the Druids.* Bk. 3. London: Charles J. Skeet, 1861.

Spencer, Craig. *Aradia: A Modern Guide to Charles Godfrey Leland's Gospel of the Witches.* Woodbury, MN: Llewellyn Publications, 2020.

Taylor, Norman, ed. *Taylor's Encyclopedia of Gardening: Horticulture and Landscape Design.* 4th ed. Boston, MA: Riverside Press, 1961.

Waite, Arthur Edward. *The Book of Black Magic.* Boston: Weiser Books, 2002.

Wohlleben, Peter. *The Hidden Life of Trees: What They Feel, How They Communicate—Discoveries from a Secret World*. Vancouver, Canada: Graystone Books, 2016.

Zalewski, C. L. *Herbs in Magic and Alchemy: Techniques from Ancient Herbal Lore*. Bridport, UK: Prism Press, 1990.

General Index

Plant Index

Adam and Eve root, *Aplectrum hyemale*, 32
African violet, *Streptocarpus* sect. *Saintpaulia*, 235
Arborvitae, *Thuja*, 163
Asafetida, *Ferula assa-foetida*, 19, 20
Asparagus fern, *Asparagus aethiopicus*, 125
Aspen, *Populus tremuloides*, 29

Benzoin, *Styrax benzoin*, 226
Boxwood, 29, 49, 52, 86–90, 147, 148
    American boxwood, *Buxus sempervirens*, 29
    English boxwood, *Buxus sempervirens* 'Suffruticosa', 29, 88
    Japanese boxwood, *Buxus microphylla*, 87
    Korean boxwood, *Buxus microphylla* var. *koreana*, 87

Carolina horsenettle, *Solanum carolinense*, 14
Cherry, 6, 49, 51, 53, 84, 91–96, 197, 213
    Kwanzan cherry, *Prunus serrulata* 'Kwanzan', 92–94
    Higan cherry, *Prunus subhirtella*, 92
    Yoshino cherry, *Prunus ×yedoensis*, 92
    Wild black cherry, *Prunus serotina*, 92

To Write to the Author

If you wish to contact the author or would like more information about this book, please write to the author in care of Llewellyn Worldwide Ltd. and we will forward your request. Both the author and the publisher appreciate hearing from you and learning of your enjoyment of this book and how it has helped you. Llewellyn Worldwide Ltd. cannot guarantee that every letter written to the author can be answered, but all will be forwarded. Please write to:

JD Walker
℅ Llewellyn Worldwide
2143 Wooddale Drive
Woodbury, MN 55125-2989

Please enclose a self-addressed stamped envelope for reply, or $1.00 to cover costs. If outside the USA, enclose an international postal reply coupon.

Many of Llewellyn's authors have websites with additional information and resources. For more information, please visit our website at http://www.llewellyn.com.